Kids' culture

Nick Harding

Thanks to Clare and the boys, and Linda Rigg for her help in the research.

Dedicated to all children's workers in Southwell Diocese – keep going!

© Nick Harding 2003

First published 2003
ISBN 1 85999 676 0

Scripture Union
207-209 Queensway, Bletchley, Milton Keynes
MK2 2EB, England
Email: info@scriptureunion.org.uk
Website: www.scriptureunion.org.uk

Scripture Union Australia
Locked Bag 2, Central Coast Business Centre, NSW 2252
Website: www.su.org.au

Scripture Union USA
P.O. Box 987, Valley Forge, PA 19482
Website: www.scriptureunion.org

Scripture quotations are from the Contemporary English Version © American Bible Society, published by HarperCollins Publishers, with kind permission from the British and Foreign Bible Society.

British Library Cataloguing in Publication Data.
A catalogue record of this book is available from the British Library.

Cover design by Phil Grundy.
Internal design and page make up by 3T Creative ltd,
Printed and bound by Ebenezer Baylis and Sons Ltd, Worcester.

Contents

Introduction

Not long ago I had an interesting couple of Sundays. The first Sunday, I went to a church that had been struggling with children's work for a while, and now had only two children left after a peak ten years ago of over fifty. The following Sunday, I was involved in an event in Manchester where thousands of children and young people were praising God and having a great time. There are real problems out there, but there is hope too, despite some of the harsh realities.

Churches throughout the Western world are seeing children flee the Christian faith at an alarming rate. There may be many reasons for this, including the standard of children's work that takes place and the low status of those who do hands-on ministry with under-11's. It may also be linked with the pattern of church activity, which makes Sundays more important than the majority of the population sees them. However, I also believe that it has something to do with the fact that in many cases churches have failed to keep up with the way the world for children has changed and is changing.

The whole point of working with children is to welcome them into the kingdom of God, but not everyone understands or sees the need. If you need confirmation of the importance of children to God, then you only have to look at Mark 10:13-16.

I hope this book helps to highlight some of the key issues that children are facing today so that you are better equipped to talk relevantly to the children you engage with from day to day. This book aims to show you the 'real world' through the eyes of under-11's. Most adults are aware that 'things aren't what they used to be', but it is important for us to try to understand the world in which our children live.

Adults have pressures and challenges to face every day. The kids' culture of our world is just as confusing for children, yet they have not learned from their mistakes and successes as many adults have. Today children face a large number of issues that at one time would have been teenage or adult problems, and they face some new ones, too. We may find the facts unpleasant or uncomfortable, but we need to take note and face up to these issues. Through the research I have undertaken, I have attempted to isolate and identify these key issues and deal with them here, chapter by chapter.

Over the last three years I have conducted a questionnaire-based survey of nearly one thousand children aged 9–11. Some were from inner-city and urban backgrounds, others from small rural villages. Some were from former mining villages facing a lack of employment and a rise in deprivation. The children answered questions ranging from 'What is the worst thing about school?' to 'What do you think about marriage?' whilst covering TV, music, clothes, fashion and career choices on the way. The questionnaires came straight back to me and were not seen or copied by teachers, parents or others in authority over the children. Many of the children's answers were predictable, some were amusing, and a number were very revealing. Their responses, along with my experience of working closely with children in both churches and schools for many years, have a bearing on the content of this book. Brief summaries of the children's responses can be read at each 'What the children say...' section. Direct quotations from the children are also displayed throughout the text.

The survey was not meant to be 'scientific' and it is not a statistical analysis of the lives these children lead. In addition, I chose deliberately to avoid issues of faith and church, leaving such things to other Christian research bodies. What I hope the results do is point us in the direction that children's lives are heading.

The questionnaire

The questionnaire the children received read as follows:

Please help me understand better what young people your age think about and do.

What is the best thing about school?
What is the worst thing about school?
What worries you about school?
What do you spend your money on?
What magazines and comics do you read?
What TV programmes do you like?
What computer games do you play?
What music do you listen to?
What makes you really happy?
What fashions and makes of clothes and trainers do you wear?
What would you change if you ruled the world?
What would you like to do as a career?
What are your views on marriage?
Would you like to have your own children?

How to use this book

The outcomes of the questionnaire have been grouped together to form the chapters of this book. We begin with the most obvious and frightening aspects of danger that face our children today. We then follow through the major aspects of today's culture, which are perhaps different to our own experiences as children, finishing with today's church.

At some points in the book you will find sections called 'Action points'. These are intended to help you think through both your attitudes to the issues raised, and how you or your church could address them with the children you come into contact with. The exercises can be done individually or with others. The action suggested may be to do more research, to think through Jesus' attitude to children, or to work through issues in your situation.

'Fact stop' sections give some facts and statistics that relate to the text. The intention is not that this book should become a research data report, but rather a readable text with a few figures to back up your knowledge.

In this book we will explore the life that many children lead; children in this context being those of school age from around 5 to 11. There are around four million such children in Great Britain. As with all issues of personal development, the examples and situations given in this book do not apply to all children from all backgrounds, but we can't ignore the fact that all children are influenced in some way by our society's culture.

While each area of culture is highlighted in a separate chapter, there is a great deal of overlap here, and nothing can or should be seen in isolation. When we think of the world we shouldn't assume it is a 'big bad world' – some things in a child's world have changed for the better. Just because this book highlights some of the negatives, which may not have been a part of our world when we were children, we mustn't lose sight of the good and the God in our world.

The Real World of Danger

I have close friends who have made a conscious decision not to have children. Their reason is that the world is too unpleasant and too dangerous a place into which to bring children. I would have some sympathy with that argument, if it were not for the fact that God is in ultimate control!

Throughout this book we will look at the world in which children now live and grow. It is a vibrant world, with many wonderful and exciting things to inspire and stimulate children. There are new ways of learning, new ways of communicating, and free and open access to entertainment and music. There is an open attitude to many things which earlier generations were afraid to speak about. Children are in many ways very safe, protected and honoured in today's world. But there are also ways in which they could be in danger. Exploring some of these danger points first will feed into some of the other issues dealt with later on in this book.

Abuse

There is no escaping the fact that children's relationships with adults can be dangerous. There are adults who want to indulge in abusive relationships with children. Much has been written on child abuse in recent years, and churches should have policies and systems to protect the children in their care as best they can. The details of what constitutes abuse and the signs to look out for have been covered in detail in other publications, and I don't intend to duplicate such detailed information here. Physical abuse, emotional abuse, sexual abuse and neglect are all forms of abuse that some children suffer. But let's remember – it is fairly unlikely that you will encounter a child who is being abused.

It is unclear whether there has been an increase in child abuse over the last ten years, or whether the increase in reporting is because the subject is much more to the fore. Agencies such as the Criminal Records Bureau have been in the headlines and raised awareness of all that is being done to protect children from adults who want to do them harm. In addition, the occasional appearance of high-profile cases of child abduction can make us think that there is a child abuse epidemic taking place.

 **Action point**

If you have suffered abuse or have been close to someone who has, you may find it helpful to go through this section with a supportive friend.

Adults who abuse children do not generally fit the 'dirty old man in a raincoat' image. They tend to be careful and convincing, and are not always male. Here are a few guidelines concerning what child abusers may be like, and how abuse can take place:

- People who abuse children and young people are usually known to their victims. They may be friends, family members, or youth group leaders. They appear to be 'normal' members of society, and 'normal' members of our churches.

- Abusers may sometimes have a caring capacity over the child (childminder, sibling, older family member) or be in some position of authority (teacher, group leader, children's worker, church leader).

- Abusers are in need and require help. They are often victims of abuse themselves, and have failed to recognise or come to terms with their own pain.

- Abusers are 90% male, and almost always older than the victim. Some may be well organised and very devious members of paedophile groups.

- Abusers come from any and all social backgrounds, and live in a range of family situations. Essentially, they could be someone who seems quite ordinary and normal.

- Abusers are known to seek out opportunities to work with children and young people, and appear very plausible.

- Abuse rarely just happens. It is often the result of a build-up of tension, fantasy and temptation, and is meticulously planned. Some abusers make long-term career or family planning decisions in order to obtain access to young people.

- The temptation to write off all men in order to protect children is very strong. However, young people need good role models and healthy relationships with older people of both sexes. Men have a vital role to play in the development of children.

Obviously, if a child is abused in any way, that child sustains damage both at the time and possibly for the rest of their life. The victim of abuse needs the immediate situation to be changed, and to feel that they are safe and unlikely to suffer in the same way again. However, they will also need a great deal of help, support and counselling, which may last for a long period of time. Social services and health services may be able to provide this. Children's workers and church leaders do not generally have the knowledge or expertise necessary to help in depth, despite their willingness to do so.

Action point

Read *Time for Action*, a report published by Churches Together in Britain and Ireland. This is an honest, open and sobering investigation into how churches deal with child abuse.

FACT stop

A pattern of abuse

A child abuser may follow a pattern that develops along these or similar lines:

1. They fantasise about a sexual act with a young person, and plan how to achieve it.

2. They minimise the potential harm and see it in terms of their own physical needs.

3. They target the victim and attempt to form a relationship.

4. They groom the child into believing that they are a good, caring and attentive friend.

5. They start to abuse, suggesting that the child caused it, must be enjoying it, and that it is the loving thing to do.

6. They bribe or threaten the child in order to keep the abuse a special secret.

7. The abuser justifies his/her actions in their own mind, and minimises the damage.

8. Even if caught, helped, reformed and counselled it is likely that the cycle of abuse will begin again. People are very rarely, if ever, 'healed' from child abuse tendencies.

Action point

Find out more about what churches can do to avoid abusive adults gaining positions through which they have access to children. Your own church and denomination should have a child protection policy and a named person responsible for making sure it is followed.

Visit the NSPCC at www.nspcc.org.uk and CCPAS at www.ccpas.co.uk

FACT stop

The British government has recently proposed legislation to make 'grooming' of children by adults via the Internet a criminal offence. The details of how this will be detected, and the level of punishment, have yet to be finalised.

Relationships are essential, usually very positive, and are only rarely dangerous. However, the rush towards exclusive relationships puts children at danger of premature sexual activity, sexually transmitted diseases, and unwanted pregnancy. Children are also vulnerable to predator adults, who target and groom children, developing abusive relationships with them. There are adults who would like to use children in pornography, assault them, or have them participate in homosexual activity. There are adults who would like to earn money from children by selling their images on the Internet or using the children as prostitutes. We must all be aware of those who could do harm to our children through relationships.

Physical and emotional safety

Homes should be a haven, a place of safety and a refuge, but occasionally they can be dangerous for children. Accidents in the home are commonplace, and generally innocent, but children are also subject to abuse at home, be it in terms of neglect and emotional abuse, or physical and sexual abuse. Homes can be very safe, happy places or sad, upsetting places, and with the rise in the number of families that disintegrate, children suffer emotional harm in the process.

Smoking

There can be few people who do not know that smoking is dangerous and can lead to death. Long and harrowing TV and newspaper advertising campaigns to make people aware of the dangers of smoking have also been used in children's and teenagers' magazines. Smoking results in around one hundred thousand premature deaths each year, and the health bill for this is massive. Children are aware of the dangers, but for many the thought of death is not something that is personal, and people who die of lung cancer appear to be old. Some young people live for the day, and don't worry about what might be around the corner.

66 I spend my money on smoking and sweets and music. 99

 **FACT stop**

It is illegal for shops to sell cigarettes to children under the age of 16, yet many do.

 **Action point**

Consider inviting an adult who is addicted to smoking to come to your church and answer the children's questions about why they started smoking, how much it costs, why they can't give it up, and what damage to their health it has caused.

Have you ever driven past a secondary school about ten minutes after the end of the school day? It is likely that, whatever the social background of the pupils, there were some who were walking home smoking. It is less likely, but still possible, that you will see some pupils from primary schools smoking.

66 I think smoking is dangerous and should be stopped. 99

Smoking is still seen as a sign of maturity, and many children smoke at an early age in order to be recognised as older, cooler, or more 'grown up'. Statistics on under-11s' smoking are not available, but figures for older children suggest that there are still significant numbers of young people who put themselves at risk by smoking, despite the cost both in terms of money and health.

The Department of Health's 1999 research project into the number of children aged 11–15 who smoke found that around 10% do so regularly. Only 2% of those aged 11 smoke regularly. More girls than boys are regular smokers, while about 8% of others questioned said they smoked occasionally. In addition, 10% of those questioned had been smokers but had given up.

No child mentioned drugs, solvents or alcohol in answer to the survey question about how they spend their money. One child mentioned cigarettes amongst sweets and CDs when describing what he spent his money on.

What the children say

Action point

Think about how you can help children understand the full meaning and consequences of 1 Corinthians 6:19: 'You know that your body is a temple where the Holy Spirit lives. The Spirit is in you and is a gift from God. You are no longer your own.'

Drinking

Some children and young people drink alcohol. There are many who are given a drop of something to drink at home, and others who like to drink at parties or when they go to a 'family pub'. Alcohol is accepted in social settings, and again some children see drinking as a sign of being grown up and mature. Even young teenagers are at risk both from the damage they can cause to themselves and others when they are out of control due to alcohol, and from addiction to the feeling that being drunk gives them. Many communities are suffering from children and teenagers drinking and causing damage to property.

In 2001 in England 13% of children aged 11 reported drinking alcohol at least once a week. 60% of all young people aged 11–15 said that they had drunk alcohol (Office of National Statistics).

Solvent abuse

Solvents are found in substances such as glue, lighter fuel and paints. Despite some restrictions on the sale of these items to children they are still used by some. The result of inhaling solvents is similar to being drunk, and can also result in a hangover. As well as the risks mentioned above, abusers can die at their first attempt by using aerosols which freeze the air passages, or by inhaling too strong a dose. As with alcohol, substance abuse can be addictive and lead to physical problems with the liver and kidneys. Solvents can also cause lasting damage to the brain.

Do you know to what extent children in your neighbourhood are buying alcohol or solvents? How can you find out?

Drugs

Illegal drugs are available in all communities to children and young people of all ages. Some schools have a particular problem with drugs, and I would dare to say few secondary schools in Great Britain are drug-free. Primary schools are also a target for drug dealers, who aim to get children young and slowly develop the level of drug dependency and addiction until they are hooked.

Drugs alter your body, your consciousness, and your ability to think and function. Some drugs are addictive and hook the user into a developing dependency. Even those drugs that are not addictive (for example, cannabis) can lead the user to rely on the feeling and state of mind they get from using the drug.

Much minor crime in the UK is related to drug use and drug dependency. Users become so desperate for another dose that they lose all notion of right and wrong, and will do anything to get the money to buy their next dose. Sadly, there are those who get their children to shoplift, or who steal cash from children in order to buy more drugs. When children become involved in the drugs scene as users it is likely that it will lead to a deeper involvement through addiction, production and dealing. These are serious crimes, and are punished by the courts. The church cannot afford to ignore the facts about illegal drug use among children, because statistically one 11-year-old in every seventeen is likely to be taking illegal drugs.

In England in 2001 42% of children aged 11–15 had been offered drugs, with 18% of these being eleven or under. 12% of the total population in that age group reported using drugs in the month previous to the survey, and 20% reported using drugs in the previous year. 6% of these drug users were aged 11, and more boys than girls were drug users. Cannabis was the most frequently used illicit drug (Office of National Statistics).

Make your church and children's workers aware of the risks of different types of drugs through training and information sessions. Support materials and help are available from www.hopeuk.org. You may also find useful information from the National Drugs Helpline, www.ndh.org.uk

Crime

There are many reasons why children and young people commit crimes. It may be due to social reasons of deprivation and peer pressure. It may be due to a poor example from family members. Some crimes can be interpreted as a cry for help or a symptom of a deeper emotional or psychological problem.

In England and Wales children are considered to be below the age of criminal responsibility until they are 10 years old. Then they are either convicted of their crime and punished in some way, or cautioned by senior police personnel.

Just because children under 10 are not considered old enough to have fully understood the criminal action they have taken, it does not mean that children do not do things that constitute criminal behaviour. There are increasing reports of police forces struggling to cope with individuals or groups of children who commit crimes and know that legally they cannot be held responsible for what they have done.

The *Guardian* newspaper reported in 2001 that 9.5 % of young children who had behaviour problems at pre-school age went on to have an adult conviction for a violent criminal offence.

Children who commit crimes are much more likely to be involved in theft and receiving stolen goods than any other crime. Damage to property and vandalism are also common crimes at the younger end of the 10–16 age group. Children under 10 cannot be charged with a crime. Those aged 10 or over who become criminals will have their crime recorded. This could affect their future prospects because, however minor their crime may be, it is still likely to result in a criminal record. Youth Courts and the Probation Service work hard to punish appropriately and do all they can to avoid the young offender becoming a regular one. Only the most serious of youth offenders will end up in a secure unit or detention centre.

Make your church aware of some of the issues around child offending by inviting a police officer, probation officer or social worker to address a meeting on the subject. Many agencies are convinced that 'diversionary activities' such as clubs and groups provided by churches can reduce young offending in the community.

In 2000 in England and Wales 0.5% of all 10-year-olds had been found guilty of a crime, rising to 1% for 11-year-olds. Boys are much more likely to offend than girls. By age 16, 6% of all boys had committed a crime, compared to 1.5% of all girls.

Dangers Outside

Some parents think that allowing children out alone is dangerous, and they therefore keep them inside, protected and isolated. There are very occasional high-profile cases of child abduction and there are also occasional assaults on children by strangers in public places, but these form a tiny proportion of the total incidents of abuse on children. Young people are also not very likely to seriously injure themselves playing in parks or playgrounds. By far the biggest danger to children outside the home is the car!

> *I like playing with cars.*
> *When I can drive I'll drive really fast.*

Road safety is a constant target of safety campaigners, and rightly so. Parents are concerned about road safety in their local area, and schools worry about the consequences of the 'school run', which sees cars full of children unloading carelessly near schools. There is also evidence that child road accident rates, including those involving bicycles, increase during the summer months when the nights are lighter and children are therefore outside for longer.

The latest figures from the Department of Transport report that over 60% of all fatal accidents involving children are the result of road accidents, with nine child pedestrians a day being killed or seriously injured. Most accidents happen between 8 and 9 am and 3 and 6 pm as children are making their way to and from school either on foot, in a car or on a bicycle. In 2000, 39,524 children aged 0–15 were injured on the road, with 191 children dying as a result of a road accident.

The Multicultural Society

Children have great opportunities to learn about other cultures and experience the diversity of our multicultural society. Schools and community groups work hard to integrate people from different cultural heritages. But there are also genuinely held views that integration at any cost is not always the right thing. A few educators are concerned that the curriculum in some schools has been weighted against Christian teaching and that the Christian heritage of the nation could be lost. This concern gives us, as Christians, the opportunity to share our faith and discover all that we have in common with other faiths. Some local councils have been accused of racism against the 'indigenous white' population, and examples such as councils changing 'Christmas' to 'Winterval' only help to cause unhealthy and unhelpful divisions. Again, we need a clear, wise and patient Christian voice, reasoning and explaining the value of all faiths, including our own.

66 *All racism is bad and should be banned.* **99**

Children do gain a great deal from living in a changing, evolving society. But there are those who take advantage of some of the more radical agendas to put forward an agenda of their own. The British National Party, formerly the National Front, now has sixteen local councillors in England and aims to add more. These councillors are elected in areas where many races mix, and the 'white' population feels disenfranchised. Children are at risk from the BNP and others who would like to influence them at an early age and encourage them to share what others describe as offensive, racist views.

Action point

Help the children in your church develop their understanding and respect for people of other faiths by developing your own knowledge so that you are able to answer their questions.

FACT stop

Children as young as 14 are recruited by the BNP and encouraged to attend camps, where they learn how to recruit others at school and in their communities.

Action point

Consider what your church can do as a whole congregation to encourage inter-faith and inter-culture dialogue, and defeat racism in your community.

Secular society

We live in a secular society, surrounded by anti-faith attitudes and teaching. 'Fundamental' has become an insult, and it is frowned upon to declare a belief in anything! Meanwhile, all newspapers have their own angle on the news and have their own point to communicate. Schools have a secular curriculum where theories (such as evolution) are portrayed and delivered as fact, in opposition to a Christian point of view. Standards in our materialistic, immoral society are not on a par with Christian teaching. The dilemma for Christians is that there is also a growing fascination, especially amongst young people, for all things 'spiritual' in the broadest sense of the word. Many celebrities will talk of their spirituality but not see it as linked in any way with Christianity or 'organised religion'.

Remember that in your children's group you are cutting across attitudes that may surround the children throughout their lives. How can you use the Bible to equip the children to stand against these pressures?

Conclusion

No one can deny that the world outside our churches can put all of us, including children, at risk. But the risks are slight compared with the opportunities to widen our knowledge and understanding, to contribute to our communities in a way that is helpful and relevant, and to serve those who are most vulnerable.

The Real World of School

Most of us would find it very difficult to look back on our childhood without thinking fondly of, or with fear about, school. For good or ill, school played a major part in our formative years and continues to influence our thinking and attitudes as adults. School is a really big issue for children.

 Think back to your time at primary school. List five really good things about that period of your life, and five things that you didn't enjoy.

In the UK there are now a large number of schools workers who are employed by either large organisations, such as Scripture Union, or local trusts to work for individual churches, or independently. They work to share the message of Christ appropriately in schools by taking assemblies, leading lessons, supporting and motivating Christian groups of pupils and students, and undertaking pastoral care work. There are many models for such work, but one key truth underpins them all: a few children go to church, a few children hang around on the streets, a few children attend uniformed organisations, but nearly all children go to school.

 Just over eight million children aged 5–16 attend school daily. In addition, 63% of all children aged 3 and 4 attend some form of daily education, usually for part of each day. Since 1998 all 4-year-olds have been entitled to free part-time education, and it is planned that this entitlement will be extended to all 3-year-olds by 2004. School attendance is compulsory for all children aged 5–16, unless parents opt for home education (DfES/Office of National Statistics).

School is the place where nearly all children can be found, at least in their earlier years. The exclusion of pupils from schools is on the increase despite financial pressures for schools to keep the children in attendance and support individuals who display challenging behaviour. There has been a sharp rise in the numbers of pupils being excluded from post-11 schools, and teachers' unions are expressing concern at the rise in poor behaviour in primary and first schools.

Home schooling

There are still a few children whose parents decide for personal, social or religious reasons not to allow them to be educated in the school system and therefore educate them at home. Home-educators often prove to be very successful with their own children, but there are sacrifices along the way too. In addition, there have to be concerns about how capable children are of relating to their peers when educated in the isolation of the home.

In a report in the *Independent* newspaper (Richard Garner, 28 January 2002), it was suggested that up to 140,000 children are now being educated at home and therefore are not in the school system, representing 1.5% of the school-age population. The leading support agencies in this field, the Home Education Advisory Service and Education Otherwise, both report an increase in parents approaching them for advice.

To find out more about home education look at the 'Home School' website at www.homeschool.co.uk. If possible, talk to a parent who has decided to educate their child or children at home, and find out why.

Christian schooling

The last two decades have seen an increasing number of 'Christian schools' as distinct from traditional 'church schools'. Christian schools are set up by Christians in a local area who are usually members of one particular church, and are outside the current state system (although this situation may be changing soon). Their aim is to teach their children a curriculum based on the National Curriculum, but from a clearly Christian point of view. At one extreme, some view such schools as exclusive hot-houses which indoctrinate pupils, while others see them as an essential move away from the creeping secularisation of the school curriculum.

Schooling today

If you were to walk into a school now, you would see some things that were familiar, and some that were most odd to you. Schools are always changing, and approaches to teaching and learning come and go almost as quickly as the latest fashions in clothes and music. Most schools now have IT areas and computer suites, welcoming noticeboards and entrance areas, and glossy brochures. All schools, even those isolated in a quiet village, are in a market place and in order to survive they need to attract as many pupils as they can. Parents are much choosier than they were in generations past, and they will pick and choose a school for their child very carefully, although not always taking into account the more important facts and figures. All of these things have an influence on pupils, and all add in some way to the pressures they face in the world of school.

66 I really enjoy having time off school! 99

Action point

Visit a school to observe what goes on and what has changed since you were at school. Due to child protection issues, schools need to be careful about who they welcome onto the premises, so make sure you have someone to introduce you to the school, and are willing to give any information requested by the school before you go in. If you already have close links with a school, try to spend time asking the more experienced teachers what they think has changed during the last fifteen years. Look out for all the good things that are now part of school life.

The meeting of two worlds

On holiday in France we were relaxing around the campsite pool when a familiar head popped out of the water. My sons looked on in horror as they recognised their headteacher from school! I am not sure who was most shocked and distressed by the experience – the headteacher or my boys!

Have you ever wondered why children hate parents going to meet their teachers? It is rarely because the teacher will spill the beans about problems with the child, because parents would have been aware of any issue at an earlier stage. It is not because they have been in trouble that day – most teachers can spot the difference between a bad day and a trend towards disruption. It is not even because parents will see the child's work for the first time, as an increase in homework means that most children work at home regularly.

For many children the only way to cope with the complexities of life is to 'pigeon-hole' their different activities. School life belongs in one box, home life in another, and so on. They like parents and carers to respect their privacy and not pry too much into what happens in their other boxes. For some children, a teacher saying 'I will ring your mother about this' holds great power, not least because it involves the collision of two areas of life.

Some children cope well with one of their own parents being a teacher in the same school, or having a teacher as a family friend. Others see their own teacher at church on a Sunday and wonder how someone so feared by pupils could possibly be a loving Christian! Whenever these worlds meet, children find it difficult and we should never assume that it is easy for them to change from calling Miss Willmot 'Lucy' at church, 'Miss Willmot' to her face at school, and 'Old Misery Cow' with their peers in the playground!

 **Action point**

Show an interest at church in what the children are doing at school. Ask about their teachers, and the things about which they are enjoying learning.

At school, children have to learn to modify the behaviour and attitudes that they have picked up from their first few years at home. They have to learn that tantrums at school do not get the results they do in the supermarket, and violence is not tolerated. They have to take on board that the racist, sexist or political opinions of their parents or family are not necessarily held or accepted within the world of school. Sadly, 'I've always told him to hit back if anyone does anything to him.

What's wrong with that?' is a common excuse used by parents for the aggressive attitude of their children. Where the two worlds meet it can be a difficult and confusing place.

Testing

One of my boys came home from school recently and said, 'We had some tests today, and I tried my best. I hope you won't be angry with the results.' I replied with the usual platitude, 'As long as you did your best, that's all that matters' but instantly I was thinking that I hoped he'd done better than his friend across the road!

Tests have always been a feature of school life at all ages. Schools and teachers need to know at what level the children are beginning their school life so that they can measure progress. Until recently those test results were internal to the school, and not always even communicated to parents. The major concern about testing in schools in England, and to a reduced degree in Wales and Scotland, is the weight that is put on those tests.

Children are tested as they enter school to find out what they can and can't do. These tests take place when the child is 4 or 5, and are often known as Baseline Assessments. As with the National Curriculum Tests that have been a feature of schools for some years, such initial assessments have a standard marking scheme and levels that the child should be at. A 'W' means they are not there, signifying 'working towards'. 'Average' pupils should go on to reach level 2 in their National Tests at age 7 and level 4 at age 11. Schools are legally obliged to publish some of the results, and 'league tables' have been used to make comparisons between schools, areas and local education authorities.

One frequently identified problem with national testing, which examines the pupils' attainment in mathematics, English and science, is that these subjects are often taught at the cost of other more creative curriculum areas. In some schools teachers 'teach to the tests', meaning that they spend a great deal of time preparing children for the content and style of the National Tests. There is little accounting for the social background of pupils or the levels of expectation in the home. If the statistics alone take over, pupils are seen as raw materials which enter and leave the 'education factory' at the same level, taking no account of their essential individuality. Creative, social and subjective developments have little space in a test-led education system. And perhaps most important of all, children can find themselves branded at the very early age of 5 as being 'average', or the dreaded 'W'.

> 66 I really hate taking tests at school — they make me scared. 99

However much tests are packaged with little activities and small group work, children know when they are being tested. They feel the pressure on them from the teacher who wants and needs good results from his pupils. Teachers are under pressure to get results, even from the most unlikely of pupils. They are not only working for the good of the pupils, they have also got the image of the school and the published results to consider. So, although children now receive a solid standard grounding in literacy and numeracy, there is less time for teachers to stop everything to watch the first flakes of snow in winter, or abandon their plans and go for a spring walk around the playing field. News-time, an opportunity for children to talk about their weekends (once a key feature on Monday mornings), has vanished from many classrooms. And children feel the pressure and tension their teachers are under. They know that their parents will be disappointed if they don't do better or at least as well as the majority of their peers. They know in their hearts that a lot seems to be riding on their work, although they don't always fully understand why.

Girls perform better than boys in National Tests at 7, 11 and 14. In 2001, at the end of Key Stage 1 (aged 7), 89% of girls reached or exceeded the expected level in English, level 2, while 81% of boys did likewise. The most interesting statistic overall, however, is that the proportion of pupils reaching or exceeding the expected level declines as the children get older (Office of National Statistics).

Make sure you are aware of when the children in your life are facing tests and exams, and pray for them. Some children enjoy the challenge, while others are all too aware that quite a lot rides on their results.

Homework

Have you ever listened to parents in the playground at the end of a school day discussing reading books? You may hear something like this:
'My David is on brown book 53 now.'
'Oh, is that all? Little Emma has moved up to yellow book 21.'

Then the pushiest parent in the neighbourhood joins in with the killer line: 'Well, my two are on free reading!'

The purpose of reading schemes, which vary from school to school, is not only to indicate how well a child can read in a technical sense, but also to indicate levels of comprehension. It helps if supportive work is done at home in hearing children read, but it doesn't help for children to be under pressure to rush through books before they are ready.

> **❝** I don't want more homework, but I think I'll get more when I change schools. **❞**

The purpose of homework is to support the work being done in schools, and to ensure that pupils understand the concepts that are being taught, without the support of the teacher. As parents are now encouraged to be involved with their child's homework, it provides an opportunity for them to find out what their child has been learning about, as well as an opportunity to positively support what their child does. But often homework becomes a competition, with the best work, most elaborately decorated, being produced more often by the parents than the child. If children make a mistake in their homework books and then correct the error it tells the teacher much more than if the work has gone through three stages of drafting, which have all been thrown away.

In the busy world of children, homework can get forgotten, ignored, or left to late at night when children do not perform well. Then it becomes another burden and pressure rather than a short and helpful challenge.

Homework seemed to be unpopular, although not universally so. Some pupils enjoyed doing homework as long as it wasn't too hard or took up too much time, while others enjoyed it at the moment but feared what it would be like the following year or in their next school.

What the children say

Action point

A number of Christian organisations support teachers and others who work in education, as well as providing information links for parents.

Visit: Christian Education at www.cem.org.uk

Care for Education at www.care.org.uk

Association of Christian Teachers at www.Christian-Teachers.org

Competition

When I was teaching in a primary school there was a premium placed on displays by one particular headteacher. She prowled the school examining displays in corridors and classrooms. Other teachers would sneak in and out of rooms, sussing out the level of the competition. I was so poor at creating displays and so desperate to earn a few 'brownie points' that I sneaked my girlfriend into school to do my displays for me!

Competition starts with the teachers, and seeps into the children. Because of the nature of schools, people want to be better than others, and certainly better than the school down the road, which takes us back to testing. There is competition and competitiveness in school, and the children know that. They are aware of where they stand on the merit or star chart; they know how many stickers they have got in comparison with their friends; they know when they are lagging behind, and they know when they are not chosen for the quiz or sports teams.

Before I am accused of being a lily-livered liberal, I must say that I think competition can be a good thing. Children need challenge, and channelled enthusiasm to succeed can take them a long way. If nothing else, the fact that any competition has winners and losers teaches children lessons about life. But competition can be damaging for some children, especially those who are aware enough to know that they will never be the best at anything. They are the ones who are always looking puzzled when the teacher says, 'So, does everyone understand?' They are the ones whose homework looks as if it has been eaten by at least three dogs. They are the ones who stand on the football pitch desperately hoping that the ball keeps well away from them. And they feel the pain of not being successful.

It works the other way too, and for some pupils this can be just as painful. There are some who know the taste of success, and know how painful it can be to have to learn that they are not the best at everything. They may be from homes with successful and pushy parents who instil in them a self-belief that defies reality. And, as the old saying goes, the higher you are the further you fall.

 Think about the work you do with children. How much time is spent in games and competitive activity, and how much on things which increase personal value and self-worth?

 Is there an opportunity for your church to support local families through homework clubs? These clubs meet after school and provide a safe venue for children to do their homework.

Punishment

I once popped in to see a headteacher friend of mine at school. As I turned the corner of the corridor, he was on his knees talking to two pupils about their behaviour. 'If this carries on I won't be able to be your friend,' he said in a quiet, calm voice to them, and they were concerned. He could have resorted to other sanctions and punishments, but his discipline style was and is about relationships, and they modified their behaviour to keep their relationship with him.

66 *I don't like getting detention.* 99

Punishment is part of any world, and is vital in the world of school as pupils develop and learn as much about social skills and structures as they do about science or sketching. Punishment does not have to be harsh or painful, and in the best schools it begins from relationship, as in the example above. The responses to punishment can vary from arrogance to remorse.

None of us likes being found out, and for some children who try hard to be good or at least portray a good image, being discovered is punishment enough. Sometimes the punishment is compounded by report cards, letters or phone calls home, mentions in assembly, or detentions. For a few this is all very bewildering, as they didn't realise that they were doing wrong in the first place, while for others it seems like overkill for a minor transgression.

Punishment in itself is not a bad thing, but we must keep in mind at all times what it is doing to the individual child. For some children, the right level of punishment will indeed act as both a warning and a reminder. It does not need to be harsh or cruel, just well-judged and suitable.

66 I hate it when I am picked on by the teacher. 99

Some children have very low self-esteem, which is reinforced by home circumstances, bullying from peers, or rejection by siblings. The humiliation of unnecessarily open and public punishment only goes to prove what they have always thought about themselves in the first place. Their opinion that they are useless, unloved and unlovely is reinforced by the punishment they receive. For any of us this is difficult, for children it is more so.

Action point

Does your church provide opportunities to support parents and families of children who display behavioural difficulties? Could you provide some 'respite care' in order to give the parents a break occasionally?

Schools work very hard to help and support children who display challenging behaviour, and they are obliged to have in place thorough and clear policies and processes. However, sometimes nothing seems to work, and exclusions are considered if the child is disrupting the education of others or putting children and staff in danger. The final sanction for any pupil at any age is to be excluded from school. Temporary exclusions can last from part of a day to a number of weeks, and generally are a sanction used by the headteacher and governing body. The cumulative effect of several temporary exclusions is that the child may be permanently excluded from school. Naturally, more children are excluded from secondary (11-plus) education than primary, but a few high-profile exclusion cases of children aged 5 and 6 have emerged. Exclusion is not always the best way of dealing with a child who finds it difficult to work within the school structure, and some children regard it as something of which to be proud. In educational terms alone, the child is likely to suffer, and is in line to do worse in exams and tests.

Teachers and other adults

I can remember two particular teachers from my first school. One was a really kind, gentle lady who drove a cool car (which I now realise was a most uncool Citroën), and the other was a strict, Sergeant-major type who wore very highly polished shoes and carried a cane around school. Strangely, I liked them both.

A good relationship with the teacher is vital to the development of every child at school. But it is not an easy relationship to get going. Younger children may never have come across another significant adult apart from a parent in their whole life, and learning to trust (let alone obey!) is a big step to take. Some children may struggle with a male teacher, having had little contact with men before and maybe also having picked up negative attitudes to males at home. There are sadly also parents who don't like the thought of their young children being taught by men.

> **"** I really like all the teachers at my school.
> They are nice. **"**

Schools are full of other adults as well as teachers, and relationships also need to be built with them. Children have to learn the names and roles of the cleaners, the caretaker, the lunchtime staff, the classroom assistants, and parents who go in to help. They have the challenge of treating them all with respect, and the pressure of trying to work out who it is worst to defy.

Teachers are, for the most part, human beings. They have homes and families, and all the usual pressures of life that we all face. They sometimes bring their problems to work with them. And they can't like everyone. It is inevitable that in every class of thirty children there are going to be one or two that the teacher just doesn't like, however professional they try to be. It is often nothing to do with the attitude of the

child, how they dress, how they behave, or the standard of their work. For a
to try their best to please the teacher but still know that they are not popular is a
tough for them to understand.

" I like Mr Wright — he is always giving Polos away! "

Very rarely personality clashes occur, and there is little that can be done but to move the child into another class if that is possible. There is no explaining why some pupils and teachers simply can't get on, and for other teachers looking on it seems irrational. Teachers who are aware that they clash with a pupil will do all they can to compensate and treat the child fairly, but in some cases it can still show. Again, the child can be left wondering what he has done wrong to be so disliked.

Consider as a church how you can support your local schools more. This can range from church members offering to help with events, to taking regular assemblies and lessons. Scripture Union, Youth for Christ and the Schools Ministry Network are among those who will help you think through the detail.
Visit www.scriptureunion.org.uk and www.yfc.co.uk

The *Times Educational Supplement* has a weekly article in which famous people — politicians, performers, and the like — write about their most influential teacher. Many put their success down to a teacher, occasionally because the teacher wrote them off and they wanted to prove the teacher wrong, but usually because the teacher was a great influence on their development and choice of career.

ey teachers come out well with many
h a high proportion naming their
and expressing concern about how
cope without them when they
o another school. Teachers were
appr...ed for their patience and the fact
that they did silly and funny things
sometimes. Continuity was an important factor, with many children liking
having the same teacher for most lessons and therefore being able to
develop a good relationship with him or her.

Action
point

As a church make sure that you pray for
and support the teachers in your congregation.
Teaching is a demanding job, with the added
burden of each teacher knowing that they
are in some small way able to influence the
next generation. Education Sunday provides
an annual opportunity to focus on schools
and children.

Tiredness

Schools are supposed to be educational institutions, yet many are becoming
social community centres too. An increasing number of schools open early in the
morning to offer pupils the breakfast that they would probably not receive at home.
But don't be deceived – this is not simply an altruistic concern for the physical well-
being of the pupils. This is a way to ensure that they are awake and well-fed enough
to be taught!

Children lead very busy lives, and can appear to come to school to have a rest. We
will look later at the outside-school activities that are now available to children and
the problems caused by freedoms, but for now we will work from the premise that
children at school are often tired.

Pupils get increasingly tired during the school day. This is reflected in the way
schools organise themselves, with maths (often known as numeracy) and literacy
being taught in the morning. In previous, less pressured times, afternoons were
much more relaxed, and free choice was a key element of the day. Up to just a
decade ago, some children aged 5 had a little lie-down at school in the afternoon.

In the current educational climate, every moment of the day is divided up into chunks so that each curriculum area gets its fair share of minutes, and slack time is at a premium. Pupils are encouraged to perform well all day, with little or no time to get their breath back or relax. This is all very tiring, and not a little bewildering.

The positive side of all this exposure to education is that children can learn a great deal, and for what they're worth the statistics do show that children are making progress at an earlier age. Many of us adults would be delighted to have been taught in the manner of the modern school.

Children struggle more when they have changed schools either due to moving house or at the end of their time at a particular school. Some school systems move children at 7 and 11, others at 8 and 12, others just at 11, and so on. While settling in to a new school, children have to try to cope with the new relationships, timetables and locations. This is enough to exhaust them, without actually having to learn anything. If they are at school for the first time they will find the first few weeks very hard physically as well as intellectually. Their tiredness can manifest itself in aggression, rudeness, lethargy, minor illnesses and displays of temper, all symptoms of being a teenager but a few years too early! For a tired child the pressures faced in the daily grind of school can be very hard to tolerate, and it is hardly surprising that when questioned by an interested adult about what they have done at school most children can only manage to muster 'Nothing!'

Bullying

As a rather small, rotund child (and not a lot has changed in adulthood!) I was subject to bullying. It was never particularly hurtful, and often meant in good humour. And I was always useful in goal when playing playground football simply because my surface area was bigger than anyone else's. I also had the advantage of older brothers, one of whom was in the army by the time I was in school. The threat of him bringing his gun to shoot all my tormentors worked wonders!

66 I'm worried about being bullied by bigger kids and made to look silly. 99

Bullying is hard to pin down, calculate and prove. It may be that the perceived problem, which is much more in the open than was ever the case in the past, is bigger than the reality of bullying. However, many children fear bullying, and some have suffered greatly from being bullied at school.

All schools have mechanisms and policies for dealing with bullying, but no school can honestly say that it will never happen. Many schools are very proactive in raising the issue with pupils, and in providing mechanisms for children to report incidences of bullying and to see things change as a result. I would go so far as to say that this is handled much better in schools now than it was in the past, and it is only because we are all much more open about the issue of bullying that it seems to be more prevalent.

Bullying often takes place out of view, with a few vindictive pupils dominating those who are weaker in physical terms, or those who simply want to keep out of trouble. At one end of the scale bullying can involve verbal 'put-downs', at the other bullies use threats of blackmail or violence to keep their victims quiet. Whatever form bullying takes, bullies can destroy lives.

A child who is being bullied can always speak to an adult, and schools will take it seriously. But the victim is aware that sooner or later the bully will know, and they fear the consequences. The common rhetoric of the bully being the weak one, and the victim being strong if they come forward is fine in theory, but for a confused child who is scared by a situation beyond their understanding it means little.

Bullying affects different children in different ways. Some children bully others because they themselves have suffered bullying, and they see it as the best way to survive. Some victims will become inward-looking and uncommunicative. Their school work will suffer, and they will struggle to make and maintain friendships. They will not admit to what they are going through even if directly challenged, and they will live their school life with a cloud hanging over them. In the worst cases of school bullying in the teenage years victims have taken their own lives.

Bullying, or at least the perceived threat of it, is an issue that worries children as they change schools. There are always urban myths about what will happen to new pupils, ranging from them having their ties cut to having their heads put down the toilet! There is undoubtedly a problem in some schools with older pupils picking on younger ones, but it is relatively rare and always dealt with by the school when it comes to light. Occasionally, there may be the problem of being a sibling of a pupil already there, with teachers calling the name and then wincing, or other pupils taking out their dislike on the younger brother or sister.

There are no obvious reasons why some children are bullied and others are not. It doesn't necessarily relate to what they wear, what they look like, or what they say. One child I know who has been the subject of serious bullying that has involved legal action is a delightful, ordinary boy, without 'victim' tattooed on his forehead. But most children still fear being bullied, and every victim goes through hell.

Bullying was a real issue of concern for many pupils, especially those about to go on to a new school. A few admitted to having suffered bullying in the past, and many feared the bullying they would face when they became the youngest pupils in a larger school.

What the children say

One child said she was always 'picked on', while others said that they were often teased.

Action point

Find out more about ChildLine, the national phone line for children to use if they have worries and concerns. ChildLine deals with thousands of calls each week. Visit www.childline.org.uk

Action point

Be open about the issue of bullying with the children in your life. Make sure that they know they can talk to you about this issue, and promise to help if you can. As hard as it seems, be honest with them about your experiences of bullying, even perhaps as the bully.

Friends and classmates are very important to the children, although a few reported having some peers in school who they would be pleased not to have around! It was also clear that others of the same age have an influence on what they listen to, wear, and look like.

What the children say

Inspections

I was sitting in a school hall recently having lunch with a group of children. One of them said, 'You're one of them inspectors, aren't you?' I admitted that I was. 'Oh, I'm not going to tell you anything bad about the teachers then!' he replied.

Many schools have developed an admirable level of school pride and loyalty. The teachers encourage the children to do their best and set a good example both in and out of school. Schools that have developed a good reputation have done so over many years, a reputation which can be lost instantly with a bad inspection report, or a report which is misrepresented by the local newspaper. The whole school community – all the staff as well as the pupils – feels the pain of a bad reputation, and the children somehow feel responsible for what the school is going through.

Most schools in England and Wales are inspected approximately every six years by the Office of Standards in Education (OFSTED). In addition 'church' schools, which are mainly Roman Catholic and Church of England schools, are inspected at around the same time as OFSTED by inspectors who look at the ethos of the school, acts of worship, and usually the Religious Education provision. The inspection does not take place in order to find fault, and the intention is not to add to the pressures already found in the teaching profession. In reality, however, the school knows that the inspection reports will be published and available to the community, and they know that bad reports can be very damaging. Often schools will pull out all the stops and put on a show, as they try to help the inspectors see everything that the school does in a brief snapshot of a few days. This puts almost intolerable pressure on the teachers and other staff, a pressure which is felt by the pupils.

Inspections do not inspect the pupils as individuals, although inspectors may look at some of their work and talk with them about it. The aims include to identify if the school has areas of weakness which are not being addressed, and if what the school says happens in policies and paperwork actually takes place in the classroom. The best way to prepare pupils for an inspection is to tell them to go about school as normal, and the best thing to do for teachers is to buy them plenty of chocolates and biscuits!

 **Action point**

Schools welcome involvement from people in their community. Some schools have 'Friends' groups, while others struggle to get people to join the governing body. There may be openings in local schools for you or others known to you.

Changing schools

In 2001 Scripture Union first produced a little book called *It's Your Move* aimed at pupils who were changing school at around the age of 11. The response to the publication was very positive, proving that changing schools is an important and underestimated issue for many children. It has been reprinted and revised a number of times and is widely available.

Children change schools at different points in their school careers depending where they live. Some move from one school to another at 7, others at 9, others at 11 or 12. There are no rules that local education authorities have to follow as to how they structure their schools, although due to the National Curriculum and national testing at 7 and 11 more areas are going over to a primary school system.

When the time comes to think about changing school most parents are now given a choice as to which school they want their child to go to. They may simply choose to let the child go on with most of his friends to the next school without too much thought, or they may visit other schools, look at crude exam results, and decide whether they like the look of the buildings or facilities. Ideally, the choice of school should belong to the pupil and parents in partnership. Parents want their children to make the best choice for the long term rather than just opting for the school where most friends are going. Children feel the pressure to do what their parents want, and may struggle to make the choice that they would prefer personally. Don't underestimate the stress involved; this can be a very difficult time for children and their parents.

Changing school is a big issue for most children whether they like to admit it or not, although learning to cope with the step into unfamiliar territory is a good lesson to learn and part of life at whatever age. Some children will step from one school to another without a moment's hesitation, while others will go through months of pain both before and after the move.

By the age of 11 the world of the primary school has become familiar, with the same teachers, a similar structure to each day, and the same building and adults within it. Children feel confident within their own school environment, knowing that they are unlikely to get something wrong or make a fool of themselves. They know that they are known by name, something which is as important to children as it is to us. The more mature pupils are able to help out in school and take on responsibilities, sharing jokes with teachers and being treated as different from the younger pupils. By the end of their time in school, they are the big fish in what is usually a little pond.

“I'm worried about getting lost and being late for lessons.”

The shock of being the little ones again is very hard for some children to cope with. The next school is likely to be bigger and noisier than the first, and they will not know their way around. The familiar, friendly teachers will be replaced by ogres who appear to be cold and clinical in their teaching and relationships with pupils. Their best friends for a number of years from their last school may be in a different class or may have gone to another school. They could also have the added problems of working out their own timetable and being taught by a whole host of teachers instead of just one or two.

Changing schools is not all bad news. Schools work hard to make the transition as easy as possible, with open days and visits to help the children get used to things. There are also things to look forward to – for example, new subjects, more facilities and more after-school clubs. Many children will have reached the point where they have outgrown their old school and are looking forward to grasping new challenges. Generally the fear children have about changing schools is far worse than the reality. For most children changing school is a very positive and stimulating experience.

Action point

Provide opportunities for children who are moving schools to relax and openly discuss what they are looking forward to, and all the good things they anticipate. For most children this will be a very positive experience, but even the most confident young people may have concerns and worries.

Some children picked up on the size of the school, especially those who were about to leave and go to a much larger comprehensive or equivalent school. They appreciated knowing their way around school, and that everyone knew everyone else. Some enjoyed being in the eldest year group in the primary school, presumably because that involved special duties and privileges. Some pupils described their schools as 'friendly', while a few commented on school dinners and lunchtime staff in a positive way.

What the children say

Action point

Look at *It's Your Move*, and investigate the possibility of your church giving copies to children moving from one school to another. You may also want to help children and parents with the earlier move into school from home or nursery, and therefore the booklets *Get ready, Go* and *Get Ready to Let Go* (both Scripture Union) will help.

Action point

Pray for some of the children in your church by name each day, asking God to be with them and help them during their school day.

Conclusion

Life at school is not always easy, painless, or successful. But for most children school is at least a good place to be, and somewhere that will be remembered in a positive light. The real world of school is life-changing!

The Real World of Relationships

We have always tried to have an 'open house', willing to have people drop in when they like. We aim to welcome friends and have people to stay with us for short or longer periods if needed. We have felt enriched by the experience of sharing our lives with many others, and feel that our children gain a great deal too as they develop relationships with a wide range of other people.

Relationships influence every area of our lives. As adults we have relationships with our work colleagues, relationships with our friends, and relationships with our families. We talk about building relationships, and think about developing relationships that may move to love and life-long commitment.

 **Action point** Make a list of all of the people you speak to during an average week. Think about your relationship with these people, and assess both what you contribute and what you gain from your relationship with them.

Children develop relationships with all of those around them, most of which are positive and helpful, and enrich their lives. Children make friends at school or at outside activities which are very helpful to them and can last a lifetime. Many children speak highly of their friends, and want the best for them.

Children see models of good and bad relationships in the home, in their communities, and in the media. They see that relationships based around sex are OK, and that abusive relationships seem to be acceptable. They see gay relationships as being 'normal', and they learn that for many people relationships come and go very quickly.

Children have to learn how to operate within the limits of their various relationships with adults. They may be able to adjust easily to the various requirements of their relationship with their teachers or their family friends, and they may be able to show respect and friendship as necessary.

Family relationships are fraught with difficulty, partly because we do not choose our families! We are landed with a group of people with whom we have things in common, and from whom we differ. There may be all kinds of problems in the family relationships of a child, which we will look at later.

Children who are still in primary school, as well as older children, are sadly under a great deal of pressure to get into exclusive relationships with others of the opposite sex. This can be healthy and helpful, with girls tempering the attitudes and behaviour of boys, but it can also be premature and damaging.

 **Action point** Make a list of all of the people you knew as a child. Try to remember friends, family, neighbours, and anyone else. Then think through what influence these people had on you as you grew up.

Unfortunately, in any work on children and relationships, we have to acknowledge the presence of adults who work hard to develop sinister relationships with children. They want to become their friends, perhaps for the relatively innocent reason that they struggle to develop relationships with other adults. Less innocently, there are adults who want relationships with children in order to abuse them.

Friends

Like most adults, I have a range of friends. Some of my friends I see a lot of, and talk freely with. Other friends live further away or have busy lives, and therefore I see less of them. I can't always remember exactly when and how these people became my friends, and some of them are very different from me. But whatever they are like and however often I see them, I need my friends.

Children need friends too. Many develop friendships at school or in their neighbourhood which last for a lifetime and are vital for them in many ways. Through peer friends children have someone to compare themselves with, someone to learn with, someone to aspire to be like, someone to match themselves against, and someone who is there for them.

❝ My best friend has been my friend for ages! ❞

Through friends children widen their circle of acquaintances and get to know other children and adults too. Through friends children get opportunities to see how other families live, chances to play with different toys and games, and even exposure to different TV programmes, music and attitudes. Many parents will testify to being concerned about some of the things their children pick up when with friends, but that is all part of growing up and learning about life.

Through developing healthy friendships with adults, children are able to mature, develop and learn social skills and communication. In the church, the role of a caring and concerned role model is vital to the spiritual development of children.

66 My friends are really important to me. **99**

We all know that child friendships can be volatile, and there are some children who know exactly how to use others to get what they want, and then drop them. Some children can be devastated when they find that their friendship has broken down and they don't really understand why. Others are hurt when they see that their friend is more successful than they are, and they feel very much the second best. We must never underestimate the pain and fear that being rejected by a friend can cause in a child.

 **Action point**   Think through what you would do if a child who looked up to you was devastated by the break-up of her best friendship. How would you care for the child? What would you say? How would you help her develop her self-confidence again?

A newer feature of today's society is that there are children who now get much more security and comfort from their friends than they do from any other people in their lives. In a world lacking in love and time, in families where there are pressures which cause children to feel left out, in homes where there is tension and fear, friends play an essential role in helping children through. In my own childhood, which was punctuated by my father spending long spells in hospital, I vividly remember the children and adults in the family next door making a special effort to befriend and support us.

66 Messing around with my friends is my favourite thing to do. 99

Children can walk into areas of grave danger through friendships. It is not uncommon for parents to explain the behaviour and attitudes of their child by saying 'he got in with a bad lot', meaning that the friends he has made have become a bad influence on him. This is inevitably going to be the case for some children, those who are 'easily led'. Gangs of children can develop, with cruel and degrading initiation rites and a strict hierarchy, and some children are destroyed in the process. Children who are able to stand against the gang are rare, and need all the support that can be offered. Teachers will often spot when unhelpful friendships are developing and try to speak to both the child and the parents. If we want to help children who are facing this challenge we must speak to them and explain the potential danger they are in, support them pastorally as a listening friend through the rejection they may face, and offer them valid and worthwhile alternatives.

Action point

Encourage the children you work with to take their friendships seriously, and to think through why they have friends. Remind them that their friendships may prove to be very valuable to them.

All the children appreciated their friends, and many in the survey said friends were the most important thing about school for them. Those in smaller primary schools also mentioned the younger children in school, and how they enjoyed being able to make friends with them and look after them. Some who were looking forward to going on to another school were concerned that their old friends were not going with them, but others positively anticipated making new friends.

What the children say

43

Loneliness

Loneliness is a feature of childhood, and perhaps it is inevitable that there will be times when children feel on their own, left out or excluded. Many children are becoming increasingly insular, sometimes preferring and often being forced to play on their own rather than mixing with others. The more young people are kept from the outside world the more they fear it.

I wonder when you last saw a group of children innocently playing on the street in your neighbourhood. Streets are no longer perceived as being safe places for children to play, with the dangers of traffic and abductors so often in the headlines. Because of the perceived dangers of being outside without direct adult supervision, there are some parents and carers who do not allow the children they look after to play outside or away from the home with other children.

> I am worried about being left out and rejected.

The implications of this are that, once inside and on their own, many children turn to isolating activities. Computer games are generally designed to be played by an individual, at their worst creating children who struggle to communicate, co-operate and integrate with peers. TVs and videos are now to be found in many children's bedrooms. As well as the dubious content of some TV programmes, there is again a problem here about integrating and learning to be part of the wider society. We will consider the content of games and videos later, but even if the content of all these was good and wholesome the child is still on their own, with no communication, discussion and support in understanding what they watch, do or listen to.

Family size has gradually declined during the last two decades, with fewer children having siblings with which to play and interact. For some children this can lead to difficulties in finding friends and developing friendships outside the home, again resulting in a sense of loneliness. Lone children are not necessarily lonely ones, and some gain much more attention and care from the adults around them, with additional stimulation and adult relationships, but they will miss out on relationships with siblings and the friends of siblings.

Action point

God's plan for humanity cuts across the separate lives that many children live. Discuss with others biblical examples of people working together and living in community. Then think how you can help the lonely children in your community and church.

Lack of love

I listened to a popular radio station the other day, and counted eleven songs in succession that included the word 'love' in the lyrics. I found myself thinking that, if love is really so popular there should not be so many lonely, hurt and damaged people in the world.

We live in a culture where 'dog eat dog', 'every man for himself' and 'look after number one' are all phrases that we hear often. Due to political attitudes and a general ethos of greed and self, corporate responsibility is played down in favour of the individual being responsible for him- or herself. In such a harsh, demanding and loveless world children can get squeezed out, feeling the rejection that results from such a self-serving philosophy of life.

Today, more than ever, children suffer as a result of this. Families are failing and falling apart. The problems in a home that is under pressure can often be centred on a parent who is not satisfied with what they have or where they have got to in life, and have decided that they want to go and find more. Just for a moment stop reading, close your eyes, and imagine the instability felt by a child whose father or mother decided that they wanted something better, so left the family behind to start a new life. Many children today feel the rejection and pain of that situation, and become scared both to give and receive love in case it is abused and ripped away from them again.

 I'm looked after by my Granny most of the time.

Today's consumerist culture has implications in that, in an attempt to get the best they can possibly have, some parents spend all their time at work, earning money and attempting to repair the damage of not spending time with the child by giving them material things. The child whose parents are too busy looking after themselves by advancing their careers and making money will suffer deprivation of some kind. The parents may have no time to play with or talk to the child, and hope that by giving lots of presents and buying material goods the child will feel loved. There are children who are developing into emotional cripples, having never heard anyone say to them 'I love you', and having never felt love that is real and without pretence.

Action point

Write one sentence that you could use to communicate the love of Christ to children.

Some children mention their family as something that makes them really happy, but for many 'family' does not get anything like the same billing as pop music, designer-label clothes, or computer games. A few mention mothers as being special to them, and others widen the family to include nieces and cousins.

What the children say

Boyfriends, girlfriends

I wonder how many of us have giggled and smiled at the sight of two toddlers hugging and kissing. How many of us smile at seeing two 7-year-olds walking hand in hand to school? How many of us would still be smiling seeing two 11-year-olds snogging and caressing at the side of the street or having sex in the local park?

It seems almost ridiculous to have a section on boy–girl relationships in a book about children, if it were not for the fact that it is a real, live issue with many children. Today they are bombarded via every form of media with images that are unhelpful, and encourage them to think that they are somehow different if they are not pairing off and developing exclusive relationships.

> **My girlfriend does things with me and makes me really happy.**

However, exclusive relationships make it more difficult for children to develop a range of healthy relationships and friendships with children of both sexes. It takes the balance out of childhood, rushing them towards adulthood when they are simply not ready. Special friendships can be really helpful, exclusive ones are not.

Children, especially girls, spend a good deal of their money on magazines which, though designed for the teenage market, are accessible to anyone. These magazines contain images of good-looking boys, often in the shower or a state of undress. They have posters of young pop stars, and offer competitions for girls to win a trip to see their hero. There are articles on relationships, make-up, fashion, kissing, sexual activity, how to get boyfriends, and so on. We will look at these publications in more detail later, but for now we have to accept that the image being given to children and young teenagers is not helpful or healthy.

“I think Blue (a boy band) are really sexy.”

The open access many children have to TV and video also reinforces the image that it is OK to have boyfriends or girlfriends, and that sex is an acceptable and normal part of life at pretty well any age. The teenage 'soap' *Hollyoaks*, very popular with children, ran a later evening series at one stage which contained much more open and obvious sexual activity. Sex is on TV all the time, be it before or after the notional 'watershed' of 9 pm.

“I like watching all the soaps.”

It is a normal part of development for children to be interested in the bodies of others. Children still play 'doctors and nurses' as a means of discovering their differences, and boys compare the size of their penis with others.

Children are getting 'older' sooner. This is a fact, and is not solely based on social factors. Physically both boys and girls are reaching the confusing phase of puberty earlier, resulting in physical development, sexual desires and peer pressure at an earlier age. While in England and Wales schools are expected to teach sex education, this is often based on physical facts, and can at times ignore the emotional side of relationships. It is no longer uncommon to hear of girls who are pregnant at 12, and there has been an increasing number of accusations of rape and sexual assault against pre-teen boys. A case of a girl aged 16 who had had ten pregnancies, the first when she was 12, was recently reported in the *London Evening Standard*. The same report commented that many girls are more concerned about keeping sexual partners than using contraception to protect their health (*London Evening Standard*, 3 October 2002). Other newspapers recently ran an interview with a boy who became a father aged 12, the child being conceived when the boy was 11. A boy of 8 I knew was caught simulating sex naked with the 2-year-old child who lived next door. One can only guess at what he had been watching or reading to give him both the idea that this is what you did and the motivation to do so. Of course, any sexual activity puts the child at emotional and physical risk. Indeed, many experts are concerned at the rise of STDs (sexually transmitted diseases) amongst younger teenage girls.

Action point Discuss with the church leadership what approach the church should take in order to help children and young people resist the pressure to get involved in premature sexual activity.

Peer pressure plays a part in the way children view their relationships with the opposite sex, as it has always done. As soon as puberty kicks in boys turn from hating girls to liking them, and other more mature boys will boast of what they have (or wish they had) done with girls. The idea is out there amongst children and young teens that 'everyone is doing it', 'it' being at one age kissing, at another touching, and so on.

66 I'm happy when I'm snogging my girlfriend. 99

(A 10-year-old boy)

Children who feel deprived of love and emotional stability may turn to others for close relationships. Statistically, girls with a deprived background and from poorer sections of society are more likely to become pregnant as teenagers, possibly as young as 11 or 12. There are children, both boys and girls, who are used as prostitutes well before the teenage years, a problem which is being identified in many areas in the UK.

The risk of becoming a teenage mother in England and Wales rises the lower the 'social class' of the girl. Girls from social class 5, 'unskilled manual', are nearly ten times more likely to become pregnant than those from social class 1, 'professional'. (Department of Health)

Consider your attitudes to children having boy- or girlfriends. Have your attitudes changed over the years? Are you convinced that sexual activity does take place between children? Would you prefer to imagine that it doesn't?

There are no figures on the level of sexual activity between children, and we mustn't assume that this is a problem for the majority of children. Thankfully, many are blissfully unaware of these pressures, and would not dream of pairing off at such a young age. The more children are active and involved with a range of friends the less likely it is that they will turn to others for exclusive relationships. On the other hand, I don't think we can afford to be complacent. Encouraging boys and girls to pair off is not a good thing, and could result in sexual activity long before the children concerned are emotionally mature enough to cope with it.

Consider the activities your church runs for children. Do they encourage children to mix, interact and be creative together? Do they encourage children to get to know and mix healthily with the opposite sex? Do they reinforce gender stereotypes?

In 2000 in Great Britain one in every ten babies was born to a teenage mother. In the same year there were 395 reported pregnancies of girls aged 13 or younger. Of these, 59.2% were aborted (Department of Health/Office of National Statistics).

The children were not asked any direct questions in the questionnaire about their relationships. However, a few girls mentioned their boyfriends in terms of what made them happy, and what they spent their money on. One boy wrote at length about how his girlfriend made him happy, another put 'snogging my girlfriend' as the one thing that made him feel really good, and others wrote that they want to meet more girls before they choose a girlfriend.

What the children say

Action point

Ask the children you know what they think about having a boyfriend or girlfriend. Let them speak openly, and try to reinforce the idea that exclusive relationships mean that other friends get left out.

Adults

Relationships with adults are very necessary and very helpful for children. They need role models to follow, adults to aspire to be like, and adults who they know care about them and love them. They need adults who are willing to give them time and attention, love and a model of maturity. There's a challenge for all of us! With the increasing paranoia about child safety and protection we are in danger of losing all that is wonderful and inspiring about children and adults growing and learning together.

Action point

Set up friendship links between children in church and older adults. The adults could be those who do not have children or grandchildren of their own. Encourage the children to speak to the adults and share with them each Sunday after the service or at another suitable time. Remember to make sure that this communication takes place in a public

Action point

place, that the adults involved are suitable, and that adequate checks in line with your child protection policy (Criminal Records Bureau for instance) have been made. Alternatively, get one of your adult groups to 'sponsor' a children's group in church. They could undertake to pray for the group, support them in practical ways, make an effort to build relationships with the children when they see them on Sunday mornings and perhaps even run the occasional event for them.

Children come into contact with many adults in their early years, from carers and health visitors to parents and the wider family. Those in churches have another group of adults to get to know, and others enjoy the leadership of adults at Cubs or Brownies and the like. Adults have a great deal to teach children through what they do and how they do it.

Children take on something of the culture of the adults with whom they come into contact. If they see adults who are caring and considerate, with a considered attitude to music, TV and the culture of the media, they will probably absorb some of it. If they see an example of godly living they will take that on too. Never underestimate the role you can have in helping a child grow and reach their full potential.

Children look to adults for leadership and example, and will quote back what they say and build their attitudes and behaviour on the example they see. Some adults can be a danger to children, as we have seen. But the fact remains that most adults who have regular or frequent contact with children want the best for the children with whom they spend time, and have nothing but their good at heart.

66 I really like all the adult leaders at Brownies. 99

Think about your relationships with children. Reflect on how much you give to those relationships, and how much you receive. And remember – you are changing lives every time you work with children!

Think of a child known to you. Make a list of all of the people the child comes into contact with. Pray for the relationships that child has, that they will be helpful, worthwhile, stimulating, and positive.

Conclusion

Wholesome relationships with peers, neighbours, friends and adults are all vital to the rounded development of a child. All relationships take work, and some children suffer in the process of developing good relationships with others. Most children, however, are able to function in relationships with many people, are not endangered by their relationships, and are not in fear of manipulation or abuse.

The Real World of Home

I wonder what your most enduring memory of home as a child is. I can remember many happy times, such as Christmas, with all the decorations and the smell of cakes cooking. I can also recall some distressing moments of sadness, fights, arguments and illness. But for me, despite some of the bad times that I went through as a child, home was a place of safety and security.

Home life is not always a positive thing for children. Home does not always represent positive experiences, and the expectation that home is a good place is not true for many children. Home can be the place where painful things happen, where there is little or no stability, or where the child simply does not want to be.

 **Action point** Be honest with yourself as you examine the prejudices you may have about family structures and home life. Remember that there is no perfect home or family, and there are many models that either work or fail.

Many children live in homes that are constantly changing, where the people in the house vary from day to day, and in some cases where the children have to live very independent lives and look after themselves. Some children become the main carers of a parent or other adult, and some find themselves taking on a parental role for younger children.

We should be cautious about making assumptions about families because of their shape. A home with both parents may not necessarily be a happy or stable environment for children, and a one-parent household may be a safe and happy place. We must be careful not to judge either the child or the parents and carers.

The majority of children probably live in relatively stable and happy homes, where good things happen and where there is plenty of love to go around. Even where this is not the case, there are organisations and agencies to help and support families going through difficult times, some of which are run by churches or have a Christian basis.

Family tensions

Home is where the family succeeds or fails. Home is where arguments take place and tensions are most obvious. Home is the place that can turn from being a haven of security to a hostile battleground.

Before we continue, I do not want to make any assumptions here. I would not want to suggest that families that go through difficult times are necessarily bad, or that it is wrong for any marriages to break up. I do not believe that home is always going to be a haven of peace and security for children, and I am convinced that sometimes when families split up it can help as well as harm the children involved. But there is an ideal here which we should at least keep in the back of our minds – the best place for children to grow up is in the midst of a caring family with a mother and a father who love each other and love the child. When things go wrong the child is generally, and unavoidably, a victim.

> **❝ I'm most happy when my family is not arguing. ❞**

The tensions that grow around families facing difficulties are picked up by children, and their behaviour can change. A child may become withdrawn or sulky. They may not perform as well at school or at other outside activities. They may try to compensate for their insecurity by becoming rebellious or defiant. As a child I went through a rough patch at school at around the same time as my father was in hospital. I had decided not to tell the teacher about my dad, and consequently she did not understand why my behaviour and attitudes had changed so much. She finally spoke to my mother about it. I had no idea that the two were connected, preferring to keep the two worlds of home and school as far apart as possible. Many parents are aware of the effect changes at home can have on the stability of their children. Many, to their credit, make a point of keeping teachers, Scout and Guide leaders, church workers and others informed.

Many children know what it is like to lie in bed and hear their parents argue and shout. They may try to hide under the pillow, or pretend that it is not happening. Some children will respond to such situations by feeling responsible for what is happening, taking on an irrational guilt.

> **❝ I really like my stepdad now, but I used to hate him. ❞**

Family tensions have a great many causes as adults as well as children struggle to come to terms with the way the world is changing. Money is often a big issue, and with rises in house prices and a modern materialistic desire to have the best of everything, parents can put themselves under a great deal of pressure. Many parents regard buying their children the best and latest of everything as a way of showing them love and care, perhaps thinking that this will replace the need to spend time with them. It is human nature to compare ourselves with those around us, and if a family does that and concludes that they are not good enough they may try to get more, have more or be more. This all adds to the stress that can cause relationships to crack.

I wish my Mum and Dad would stop fighting.

Action point

Think of your own family. List the top ten things that cause tension in your home. Reflect on what effect these tensions may have on others close to you.

FACT stop

In 2001, 20% of children were living in a family with a lone parent, an increase of 8% on 1991. This means that 80% of children live in a household with two adults. Statistically, children from black, black British or mixed race backgrounds are more likely to be in one-parent families than children from other backgrounds. These figures are not static, and are changing all the time. Children are living in an increasing variety of different family structures. Due to changes in cohabitation, marriage and divorce patterns, children may experience a range of different family structures while growing up. Parents separating can result in one-parent families, and new relationships can create stepfamilies (Office of National Statistics).

Family splits

Up to 50% of children may experience their families breaking up and parents divorcing. If the family is in turmoil or one of the parents is abusive then the end of the relationship may be a good thing in the long term, but it still affects the child. Again, children may demonstrate a range of uncharacteristic behaviours and attitudes that will draw the attention of the adults around them.

> Marriage is stressful and painful. I don't want to get married.

The emotional confusion many children feel as their parents go through a divorce or split is known to run deep. Most parents want the best for their children, and many painful and unhappy marriages have continued 'for the sake of the children'. But there are also children who are used as emotional pawns in the game of divorce, and are asked to make difficult and confusing choices. There may also be involvement with the legal system, social workers, and others who are seeking the best for all concerned. However hard everyone works to protect the child from these unexpected and strange diversions, they can be frightening and confusing.

> I feel happiest when I go to see my Dad.

Some children have got used to living in two homes, sharing their parents and grandparents, and making the most of the situation. There are a number of arrangements, including parents sharing custody on an equal basis and children therefore living in two homes, to one parent having full custody and allowing the other some hours each week or fortnight with the child or children. A great many children are happy with the situation they face, seeing it as being 'normal', or at least normal for them. One boy of 8 who effectively has two homes said this: 'It's great! I can get everything I want from Dad at the weekend, and everything I want from Mum during the week. I've got more than my friends!' Other children find the sense of being split or torn very painful, and often feel responsible in some way for what has happened. They may be picking up negative feelings about one of their parents, or told things which are not true or are not easy for them to understand at a young age.

Almost nine in every ten stepfamilies consist of a couple and at least one child from the female partner's previous relationship (Office of National Statistics).

The way children see and experience 'family' has an impact on the way adults speak to children and the language used. For some children today our talk of a 'loving Father' means nothing but pain. The use of words such as 'parents' and 'home' are not universally accepted as words of comfort and care. For some 'uncle' means a family member, while for others it means the man who is living and sleeping with Mum at the time.

There are many Christian organisations that work to support children and families, and provide links to other agencies and resources.

Visit:Good News Family Care at www.gnfc.org.uk

Care for the Family at www.care-for-the-family.org.uk

Kidscape at www.kidscape.org.uk

National Family and Parenting Institute at www.nfpi.org.uk

Discuss with others how your church could help families and parents work through the difficulties they may have, and come to terms with the break-up of the relationship if there is no way to repair the damage.

In 1961 there were 27,000 divorces in England and Wales, a figure which had risen to 154,628 by 2000. In 1999 there were 147,721 children aged under 16 involved in their parents' divorce, producing an average of one child involved in every divorce. Of those, 37,706 children were aged under 5, and 66,442 were aged 5–10. The 5–10 age group therefore has a higher instance of parental divorce than younger or older age groups.

Despite the fact that at least 30% of the children will have been part of families that have experienced splits and difficulties, most children were keen on getting married and some wanted to have children too. Some children felt that it was a bit early to think about

What the children say

'that stuff', and others were quite emphatic in their negative responses, describing it as 'disgusting' and 'gross'. Another boy responded, 'Probably yes, but ask me again after sex education!'.

Action point

Consider families in the Bible. What do the stories of Abraham and Isaac (Genesis 22), Jacob and Esau (Genesis 27) or Joseph and his brothers (Genesis 37) have to teach us about families?

Support at Home

Some children know that they can turn to their parents for help with decision-making and advice. Despite children being young they do feel many pressures, and have decisions to make. As adults we may see the turmoils they go through as trivial or naïve, but for children their feelings of confusion are all too real. Some children get a lot of support at home, with parents who are willing to stop everything, listen, and give advice. Most of all such actions give the children their own mechanisms to weigh up the options they face and make good decisions for themselves. Other children receive very little help and support in making decisions, and do not feel they can turn to their parents for advice.

66 I tell my Mum things, but my Dad just gets angry with me. 99

Discipline

Discipline in the home may take place too harshly, or not at all. Children present challenges to parents all the time, and there is no easy answer to the question 'How should a child be disciplined?' There is now a growing reluctance to smack or physically punish a child, and many parents fear being accused of being bad parents or abusers if they do so. Certainly there is a strong argument that to smack a child is to misuse the power and authority you have over him or her. But discipline of some form in the home is necessary. Children who live with no discipline at home will expect to behave in the same way in other areas of their lives. They will struggle to interact and develop relationships, they will expect to have everything their own way, and they will fail to fit into social structures and norms. Children who live with too much discipline in the home may also have problems outside. They will carry a sense of fear and guilt with them, and worry about the consequences if they do anything that may be disapproved of by their parent. Discipline is often an issue which causes problems and tensions between parents, again leading to children developing a sense of guilt and responsibility for what is happening.

Sickness and death

66 I was really upset when my Nana died. Nobody told me what was happening. 99

Attitudes to illness and death can confuse children. I was brought up at a time when it was thought harmful for children to attend funerals or to be told about death honestly and openly, and it was always something of a scary mystery to me. I have tried to be much more open with my children, and when my father died they took it all very much in their stride. Death is a fact of life, yet many families shy away from the issue, which has been called the one great taboo of our generation. Thus some children spend a great deal of time grieving without really knowing what has happened. Some may be expecting the one who has died to come back after 'going away' or be thinking that he or she has turned into an angel watching over the home, depending on the view or the story given by the adult they talk to at the time.

Find out what your church says to children who have suffered the death of someone close to them. Make sure that children are not being patronised or offered false hopes.

The clash of cultures

Children suffer when the attitudes in the home clash with those in the outside world. This may be as simple as the time children go to bed or the music they are allowed to listen to. Alternatively, the child who is told, 'If anyone hits you make sure you hit back' may be in for a great surprise the first time they put the advice into action at school! The clash of standards and attitudes is a particular problem for children from Christian families, who in so many areas seem to be standing against a tide that is rising fast. Attitudes to TV programmes, games, raffle tickets, the lottery, sex education, Hallowe'en and a whole bagful of other issues can mean that children have to think through how what their parents say is not the norm for all adults.

Many children find themselves in trouble when repeating or living out the attitudes they have absorbed from home. In our culture of many cultures, racism is still significant, and is evident in the playground as well as on the football field and street corner. Some children are 'innocently' repeating words or comments that they have heard at home, without realising that their attitudes to others' race or religion are hurtful and inappropriate. Some British nationalist political organisations even run youth camps for children and young people in order to nurture racist and homophobic attitudes.

Action point

Parentline provides support for parents who are facing problems or seeking impartial advice. Tel: 0808 800 2222.

Make a list of the top ten attitudes you hold as a Christian. Then think through how contradictory these may seem to children who are brought up in homes which hold to different standards. Here are a few examples:

Keep forgiving those who cause you pain.
Put others before yourself.
Don't be jealous of what others have.

Relationships at home

I have always thought it strange that, despite the fact that they have an incredibly significant impact on all of our lives, we do not get the chance to choose our families. If we did I really wonder how many of us would have chosen the same people!

Some children simply do not get on with their siblings. This is not a particularly new situation, although with the advent of many more second families and remarriages there are stepsiblings and half-siblings to be contended with too. There are children who feel a strong and long-lasting sense of rejection when a new little brother or sister comes along, or when the attention of a parent has to be shared with the new ready-made family of Dad's girlfriend. On the plus side, in many families of many forms the children do get on well and care deeply about each other.

66 My little brother makes me really happy, because he's funny. 99

Physical, emotional and sexual abuse and neglect are all features of some homes, and experiences some children go through. We shall not dwell on this subject at this point, but we must remember that most children who are abused suffer at the hands of people who know them well, often in the home situation. This may be a parent or step-parent, uncle, babysitter, or family friend. Occasionally incest also takes place between brothers and sisters.

Most children cope well with change, and many thrive surprisingly well with changes to the members of the household. The reality of home life for some children is that they have to get used to different adults in the home, including adults who come and go as relationships between parent and boyfriend or girlfriend fail. Sometimes bonding will take place, while other children will have trouble getting to know and like the new adult in their life.

A teacher was pleased to see a rather sad boy smiling as he walked into class one morning. The boy's home life had been rocky over the last couple of years, and he had had little to smile about. 'You look happy,' said the teacher to the boy. The boy's beam grew as he answered, 'Yes, we've got a new Dad at home', and he went on to name the man concerned. A girl at the back of the class overheard the conversation and shouted out, 'Oh yes, we've had him. He's good!'

Favouritism and inequality are common problems that children face in the home environment. There are numerous theories about who wins and loses in the lottery of relationships at home. It is often thought that girls have a better relationship with their fathers than their mothers, raising many issues when marriages and families break up. A mirroring theory is that boys get on best with their mothers. In terms of the position of the child within the family there are also differing views. Some say the eldest child loses out, while others believe that a middle child is excluded. There is a theory that a youngest child feels like an after-thought, a theory which, as the youngest of four children, I would heartily support. There is research evidence to back up and refute all these theories, but needless to say some children do feel rejected and left out in the home and within the family. Homes are rarely totally fair places, reinforcing what children will find in other areas of their life – life is just not fair!

66 My Mum likes my sister best. 99

Some children as young as 6 have to work at home in the role of carer for a sibling or parent. For some of these children the situation may be temporary as a parent recovers from hospitalisation, but for others it could be a permanent situation to which they have to adjust. However, the burden of taking on adult roles and responsibilities in the home can have a negative effect on the child's performance at school, development, and health. They may find that developing friendships is much more difficult as they do not have the time to devote to 'childhood' things. They are losing out on the freedom and enjoyment that is usually part of being their age.

Find out more about people who are the main carers of others, particularly those children who care for their parents or siblings.
Visit Carers UK at www.carersonline.org.uk

The Children's Society estimates that 51,000 children aged between 8 and 17 are currently caring for others in the home. 71% of young carers questioned reported being bullied at home, and 60% live in one-parent families. The average age of young carers is 12, but the Children's Society has worked with young carers as young as 5 (Children's Society).

Carers, babysitters and childminders play an increasingly important role in the lives of many families. In my home we are blessed with the frequent presence of someone who acts as an additional grandparent to our boys, and does much more than keep an eye on them. In the busyness of our lives she is absolutely essential and literally a gift from God. Best of all, she sees the work she does for us, though paid, as ministry too. I am absolutely convinced that the lives of our two boys have been greatly enhanced by her love and support for them and us as a family. That said, carers can become replacement parents for some children, and have a greater influence over the development of the child than parents. This may cause clashes over behaviour, morality and other attitudes.

Action point

Consider developing and providing a parenting course for people in your community, including members of the church who think they don't need a parenting course!

Parents delight in the successes of their children, and want them to do well, but there are also some parents who want to relive their lives through their offspring. The pressure to perform can become overwhelming for some children, who desperately want to do well to please keen parents, and fear failure. There is no doubt that children in this generation have more opportunities to learn and succeed than ever has been the case in the past, but that does not give parents the right to attempt to live their children's lives for them!

> **I like seeing my Dad at weekends — he buys me things.**

I wonder how many of us feared one parent more than the other when growing up. The creation of 'goody' and 'baddy' parents is very easy. I have heard myself say, 'Wait till mummy gets home' more than once, and I regret it. It is not helpful that children develop an unbalanced view of their parents or carers, seeing one as the disciplinarian and the other as 'soft'. For some children an added confusion comes about when they spend a small amount of time being 'spoiled' by their non-custodial parent, and then have to behave in the manner expected by the parent who has to carry the lion's share of responsibility.

Many parents are under a great deal of pressure to cope with all the demands of home, work and life in general. They may find it difficult to make time for their children, or the time they do offer is rushed and stressed. Yet most parents are at least striving to do the right thing, and when push comes to shove will stop and give attention to their children.

Action point

Think about some of the children you know, and make a list of their varied home situations. Reflect on how your work with those children could be adjusted to accommodate some of the baggage they carry.

Abbey National surveyed 965 parents to find out how much time they spend with their children. Despite packing in more activities per day, parents now spend more time with their children each day than was the case forty years ago.

Does your church have a strategy for supporting and helping families in crisis in your community? What do you think you could do to support and serve those who are finding running a home and parenting difficult?

Conclusion

For most children home is a wonderful, safe and happy place. For some it is a place of tension and fear. For the majority home is a mixture, with good times and bad times. This is the real world of the child at home.

The Real World of the Media

The world has changed, and it continues to change fast. Perhaps one of the reasons for this is the instant nature of the media. There is instant news from all around the world, real-life drama is played out in the press and on screen for all to see, and nothing is either unsaid or unseen. The media has twenty-four hour access to every corner of the world, and 'openness' is the order of the day. We can all watch what we like, and there is no 'taboo' subject left.

Many teachers and others who work with children have long been concerned that what is seen on TV or in videos is accepted as being real. Even adults reported a strange realisation that the images of the 11 September 2001 terrorist attack on New York were real. Adults can assimilate the information and work out truth from fiction, even if both look the same. Children cannot always do likewise.

If you had a little child you would not feed him food without checking it to make sure it was suitable and at the correct temperature. Yet we allow children, our children and the children in our communities, to feed on material churned out by the media, which is at best tolerable and at worst damaging and harmful.

In 1999 a survey of time spent watching TV found that children aged 4–15 watched an average of eighteen hours of television each week. This is live TV viewing only, and does not include time spent watching videos or DVDs.

TV and Films

The television has been accused of many things in its long history. It has been accused of destroying family life and traditional meal times, and inhibiting conversation. It is said to have brought a new morality into the home, showing things and demonstrating attitudes which are not acceptable to some or many. It is supposedly responsible for much violence in society, and some accuse it of encouraging 'copy-cat' crimes, while making others scared of the perceived level of violence, which is much higher on television than in reality.

66 Horror films are my favourites. I watch them in bed at night. 99

On balance there is some truth in all of these accusations, but before we jump to conclusions and throw our TV sets out of the window we must consider this issue more. After all, TV is not all bad, and whether we like it or not, it is a window on society as a whole. Each TV set comes with an 'off' switch, and if we really are concerned about what is being viewed we can switch it off or even join the 5% of households in the UK who do not own or use one. Television programmes reflect, to some extent, what is going on in the world outside, and are therefore like a mirror to the society we have made. The soaps are designed to condense events and storylines in order to have more happening than would normally be the case, and therefore there is a sense of unreality there. But still these things do happen. If we don't like what we see we can hardly blame the messenger!

Children are affected by the TV programmes they watch. With an average child watching just under three hours of TV a day, and many watching a great deal more than that, they cannot help but see things that are not ideal viewing. Given that many children have access to a TV in their own rooms, away from parental control, we can and must assume that some are watching programmes well after the 9 pm 'watershed'. But even programmes screened before the watershed are not always suitable. Children's programming has changed a great deal since the early days of innocent puppet-based shows and the beginning of *Blue Peter*. Programmes are now very bright, attractive, and hyped-up. Noise and colour, fast action and quick visual image changes are all standard features of a children's show. There is a mix of cartoons, live action, and still a few factual and even 'educational' programmes such as *Art Attack* and *Newsround*. On Sunday mornings programmes can be found hidden in the schedules which have religious themes, such as *The Ark* featuring puppets who travel around and find out more about the major world religions. There are also a great many imports from the USA, often teen dramas based in school settings. Through satellite and cable, some children now have access to sixty or seventy channels, including specialist children's channels. This is a heady mix, and amongst the gold is some dross.

Action point

Watch as much children's programming for a week as possible. Make a note of the programme title and mark it with the following in mind:

Action point

Would it be helpful for a child to watch, reinforcing moral values or educating them in new things?

Was it pure fun?

Was the programme unhelpful in any way?

Cartoons used to be seen as a medium for children. There are satellite and cable digital channels that are predominantly cartoon channels, such as *Cartoon Network, Nickelodeon* and *Fox Kids*. With the advent of adult cartoons such as *Beavis and Butthead, South Park* and *The Simpsons* we would be wise not to assume that cartoons are all aimed at children and contain innocent messages. Those mentioned above are often not suitable for children, although there is an argument in favour of many elements of *The Simpsons* being sound, moral, and realistic.

But children's cartoons should also come in for scrutiny. Some are violent, displaying death and destruction as commonplace and 'normal'. One popular cartoon, *Pokemon*, carries such themes. There is much anecdotal evidence that younger children often play out what they see in action cartoons, only to discover that when they jump out of a window they do not always land on two feet without breaking any bones. Many a teacher will tell stories of children kicking each other violently in the playground, and then being stunned that it actually causes real pain.

Action point

Ask a group of children you work with what films they have seen recently. Ask them if they know what rating (U, PG, etc.) those films had, and if they thought they were good films to watch.

All children mentioned programmes that were popular with them. Many enjoy watching cartoons, including 'adult' cartoons such as *South Park, God, the Devil and Bob*, and, of course, *The Simpsons*. Other popular

What the children say

programmes include *Sabrina the Teenage Witch, Angel* and *Buffy the Vampire Slayer.* Other less popular programmes were also mentioned, including late-night comedy (*Smack the Pony, Eurotrash, Trigger-Happy TV*) and dramas such as *Jonathan Creek, Casualty* and *Holby City.* A few children mentioned wildlife programmes, two out of over nine hundred enjoyed watching the news, and many boys enjoyed sports programmes, especially wrestling and football.

Dramas aimed at children are often very well written and produced, and do help them through some of the issues they face by carrying storylines that tackle those issues. Nevertheless, there may be moral issues that Christians would find unwholesome, and a level of political correctness which dictates that anything goes, anything is acceptable, and anything is right if it feels right. Children's TV dramas have covered issues such as gay relationships, child abuse, sex, depression, smoking, alcohol, drugs and incest. These are all great issues to be tackled and clearly reflect the world around us, but are not always handled in a biblical way.

Action point

Visit your local Christian bookshop and look at the range of videos and DVDs that are produced for children, many of which are American. See whether there are programmes and films suitable for the children in your church to view, but watch them yourself first.

Many TV dramas and films aimed at the teenage market have occult and spiritual themes, and even the more innocent programmes such as *Blue Peter* and *Newsround* feature editions on ghosts, Hallowe'en, and so on. Programmes such as *Angel, Charmed* and *Buffy the Vampire Slayer* are currently in vogue, and as they pass into obscurity others will come along. From the light humour of *Sabrina the Teenage Witch* to the dark frightening themes of Buffy, there is a message that not only is there a spiritual dimension to life, but that dimension is in some ways exciting, fascinating and gives power and knowledge. It is true that good always wins out in the end, but the 'good' that wins is not the 'good' of a loving God.

66 Buffy is my favourite programme, but it's creepy too. **99**

Adult programmes

Many programmes on TV are not designed for children, and are certainly not ideal for children to view on their own. Even relatively innocent programmes such as the home video show *You've Been Framed* have undertones which are not altogether wonderful! This programme features the misfortunes of others, with things going wrong, items breaking, and people falling over. It is hard not to laugh at these clips, and easy to forget that each of those people is real and may have been hurt or humiliated by the incident. To revel in their pain seems in some ways to demean our humanity and concern for others.

Police dramas are popular both with adults and children. Some have detectives sorting out crimes in short series or one-off programmes. From time to time detail is graphic, fear is very well illustrated, and horror becomes very realistic. *The Bill* also operates as a soap opera, and therefore has storylines about the characters who appear regularly. Recently the stories have included two gay police officers kissing, and the introduction of a lesbian officer. All this is portrayed as being perfectly acceptable behaviour, and screened at 8 pm.

66 My favourite TV is Bad Girls and Ali G. **99**

The storylines followed by many adult programmes are often complex and reflect life under the microscope. They have adult themes, adult morality, adult behaviour, and adult content.

Films are now readily available on video or DVD, and many families have a good collection of films. They all come with a certificate indicating the age that viewers should be. However, there are many children who have access to unsuitable films with horror, violence, death and sexual activity. Younger children are prone to bad dreams as their imaginations run riot with all of the frightening images they have seen. Older children get an idea about the way that people can behave, which on the surface looks glamorous. Other films are thought by some to encourage a fascination with the occult and things of evil, and to open a gateway to unhealthy activities.

Soap operas

Soaps are popular with children. They provide a degree of continuity from day to day and week to week, and often have clearly-defined 'goody' and 'baddy' characters. Soaps can become, for many viewers of all ages, a second family or alternative group of friends. But the most popular soaps with children are not those we might expect them to enjoy, such as the Australian imports *Home and Away* and *Neighbours*. Dramas that have a 'soap' element, such as *Casualty* and *Holby City*, were mentioned by some children. But in my research the most popular soap, and indeed the most popular TV programme overall with 10- and 11-year-old children of both genders was *Eastenders*.

 **Action point**

Always view a film or video before showing it to children. If there are sections that you are not happy with, fast-forward through them and fill in the story yourself.

Soaps are overwhelmingly popular with children. *Coronation Street, Home and Away, Hollyoaks, Neighbours, Emmerdale* and *Brookside* all get mentions. *Eastenders* is the most popular of the soaps.

 **What the children say**

The soaps aimed at a younger market such as *Neighbours, Home and Away* and *Hollyoaks* revolve around themes of love and relationships. Bad things do happen, although they usually come right in the end. Love and sex are portrayed as natural things to get into, and nearly all of the younger characters are very attractive. Make-up helps cover up teenage acne, and good dentistry gives all of these beautiful young people perfect white teeth and amazing smiles. These soaps are enjoyable to watch, and as long as children realise that it is all a fantasy dreamed up to keep them watching then there is little wrong in it. But as soon as young people start to crave after the characters, meet someone like them, or even become like them, then it becomes a little dangerous.

Keep a notepad near the TV 'zapper' and note down the names and content of programmes that are screened before 9 pm which you think are unsuitable for children to be watching. If you feel strongly about a particular subject matter or storyline, ring or write to the broadcaster concerned. Every complaint is noted, and taken to represent the views of hundreds and in some cases thousands of others.

It is difficult to think of *Eastenders* as a programme for children, yet many children watch it and follow the storylines with interest. It is by anyone's standards a dark soap, and contains a view of reality that many people find depressing and disturbing. The story themes expose children to the more negative side of reality, including relationship-hopping, abuse of various kinds, domestic violence, and drink and drug problems. *Eastenders* may have a place in helping children as well as adults come to terms with what can happen and does happen to some people, but it needs to be handled with care.

> *Eastenders is my favourite soap. I want to be an actress in it one day.*

Comedy

Some of the children reported viewing comedy programmes which, again, are principally aimed at an adult audience. Many of those mentioned are on TV very late at night, and contain content that is not suitable viewing for children. *Eurotrash* is a strange mix of Euro-pop acts and reports on people or situations that invariably have something to do with sex and nudity. For this programme to be mentioned alongside *Blue Peter*, *Eastenders* and *Sabrina the Teenage Witch* demonstrates that for many children the lines are so blurred as to be non-existent.

The children mentioned 107 different TV programmes. 32 were programmes made for and aimed specifically at children. 48 were programmes made for a general or adult audience and had a mid-evening or weekend slot. 27 were programmes that have a post 9 pm slot, and are made specifically for adults.

What the children say

Music videos

Music channels such as *MTV* and *The Box* broadcast wall-to-wall music videos plus advertisements for albums and videos. A pop song that aims for a chart position has to have a bright, lively and attractive video. Many children enjoy watching the videos and can tell you what they are like. In 1999 Britney Spears was criticised for setting a video in a school and being dressed in school uniform while singing and dancing in order to attract older male fans.

Music videos are as lively and memorable as possible in order for people to connect the visual image with the music and therefore go out and buy the single. But many of the videos are of images which, again, many Christians would find distasteful and inappropriate. Images that feature prominently include dancing, often in revealing clothing, bed scenes, and plenty of kissing. It doesn't take much imagination to work out what is being portrayed, even though certain limits of taste and decency are imposed. When the video does 'cross the line' of taste and decency it gains much valuable publicity.

66 Robbie (Williams) is good looking. I've got lots of posters. 99

Like many films and TV programmes, especially those aimed at the younger market, music videos always feature 'beautiful people'. These ultra-perfect people must exist, but they don't relate to the circumstances of the lives that children lead. The people singing, dancing, or acting out the storyline are attractive and without a blemish. They are often in expensive and attractive settings and scenery (money is certainly no object for video producers and record companies). Love stories always run smoothly, and the message that true love is easily attainable with some wonderful man or woman is clear. There is nothing wrong with watching a dream or even experiencing one, but when this becomes a reality which a child thinks they can attain it is another matter.

Watch some *MTV* or another music channel, and make a list of the videos which you think are and are not suitable for children to be watching.

Music

There are bands and musicians who are designed, packaged and targeted directly at the child and teenage market. The winners and runners-up of pop-star competitions and talent shows are hugely successful and popular with young children. They are packaged to be attractive and are given clean images. The publicity managers who aim for this market with their 'product' singer or group are relying on a strong selling point – 'pester power'. They know that if the product is attractive enough children will nag and pester their parents to give them the money to buy the CD, poster or calendar. But there is nothing new in all this. We can think back to the nineties and the way Take That and The Spice Girls became hugely popular on the back of a very young following. In the eighties Wham! did the same; in the seventies there was the Bay City Rollers, and even the Beatles in the sixties. Perhaps the only difference is that the fans, those with money to buy the products, are getting younger.

Purchase copies of *Smash Hits* and *Top of the Pops* magazines. These feature the lyrics of some of the most popular songs currently in the charts. Read the words to find out what children are listening to.

There are many issues about the words and meanings of songs that have been raised by those working with children and young people. Some rap acts are accused of having racist, sexist or homophobic words and attitudes in their lyrics. Some American rap acts have been accused of inciting domestic violence against women, and the drugs and gang culture of some acts has led to shootings amongst performers. There is a question here about the kind of role models that children aspire to be like.

Often CDs carry a warning sticker advising that the words of the songs may be offensive to some in terms of the message or the foul language used. These are very attractive to younger purchasers, who want to listen to such music in order to appear 'grown up', daring or rebellious. Many people have been concerned for decades about the darker side of pop music, and are able to use some heavy metal bands who dress in satanic-looking costumes as examples of evil music. This music gets into the minds and imaginations of young listeners, and opens them up to unhelpful influences.

Popular music became a big phenomenon in the fifties, around the time when the word 'teenage' and its associated concept was taking shape. Pop groups and acts come and go, some courting controversy and others trading on a clean image. The Eminem of today will be followed by someone else with distasteful lyrics and entrenched views. The hard-hitting, aggressive Limp Bizkit will be replaced by another similar band. It is even possible that the young, attractive, hugely popular and reportedly Christian Gareth Gates will pass into obscurity and be replaced by another such. But as the names come and go the themes, language, packaging and manipulation of young people remain the same.

What the children say

Music is popular with children, with only a few reporting that they didn't listen to any music. Popular acts with girls include Robbie Williams (whose video for 'Rock DJ' featured something akin to a striptease), Craig David and Britney Spears, and a whole range of singing and dancing groups including Westlife, Blue and the now split Hear'say. Both boys and girls listen to Shaggy, whose hits are usually about sexual relationships and had a recent song in the charts entitled 'Sex Machine'. Boys often listen to heavier groups including Limp Bizkit, Linkin Park, Offspring, and Green Day. Some reported enjoying heavy metal, hard rock and club music. Many children enjoy listening to the controversial rapper Eminem. There were, as always, a few exceptions to the rule. One child likes listening to Frank Sinatra, while another enjoys Irish music.

Look at Psalms and Proverbs in the Bible, and list any passages that instruct the reader about how they should spend their time.

Magazines

There are many magazines and comics on the market aimed at children and young people. They range from specialist magazines on computers, weapons and cars, to comics such as *The Beano*. There are many glossy magazines aimed at girls and teenagers, and available to all.

Comics are still there, hanging on to a smaller market share. *The Beano* is still popular with children, although the age of those who read it has slipped a little. *The Beano* is full of slapstick humour, with a little streak of vindictiveness every now and again! It follows a similar theme to many Roald Dahl books, which is to see adults fail and being humiliated. Many of the characters in the comic have been there for many years and generations, and are well-loved by adults. *The Beano* used to be read by boys, while girls liked to read *Jackie. Jackie* was closed in the nineties after failing to keep up with many of the magazines aimed at teenagers but read by younger girls. At the time one journalist wrote that *Jackie* had to finish because she 'would not lose her virginity'.

66 *Beano is my best comic. It is funny and makes me happy.* 99

Many of the magazines for girls are read by children much younger than the target age, with *J17* (formerly *Just 17*) being read by girls aged 10 or younger. Boys also read some of these magazines, and one or two even have a page aimed at boys.

Most of the girls reported reading at least one magazine, some aimed at the teenage market and others which feature pop stars and music features. Popular titles at the younger end of the age spectrum

include *Mizz, Girl Talk, Blush* and *Sabrina's Secrets*, while at the older end of the market many girls regularly read *Bliss, J17* and *Sugar*. Pop magazines include those brought out by specific bands and singers as well as *TOTP, Smash Hits* and *TV Hits*. A few girls bought special interest magazines on horses, riding, sport and fashion. Boys were generally much more into special interest magazines and bought magazines on wrestling, football, sport, cars, airguns, Formula One, Playstation, skateboarding, and a number of other sports and activities. Only one girl reported reading *Woman* and *Woman's Own*, and one boy mentioned *Playboy*.

Action point

Purchase a range of children's and young teenage magazines. Highlight them in three different colours, marking the items that are positive for the children to read, those that are OK – neither helpful nor harmful, and those that are unhelpful.

Many of the pop music magazines, and all those aimed at girls, feature those 'beautiful people' we mentioned earlier. Again, we see perfect, well-groomed teenagers and adults portraying an image that is far from real. Fashion articles and shoots have the very best of clothes, and young people as models who are particularly attractive and slim. The photographs of pop stars and bands are, as you would expect, designed to show those concerned in the best possible shape. Even those magazines that have photo 'vox pops' with pictures of boy or girls making comments seem to manage to find those without a spot of acne or a gram of extra weight. All through these magazines the unspoken message is that how you look really matters, and ideally you should look like someone in the photos.

66 Sugar is fun to read. It's my big sister's. 99

The photographs used often portray a sexual message. Some of the magazines aimed at the older end of the market have pin-ups of boys and young men who are in the shower, getting changed, or have forgotten to do their trousers up! They are the pictures that make it onto the walls of girls' bedrooms, and portray an image of male perfection which most girls won't get near to except in their dreams. The sexualisation of everyone from pop singer to TV actor turns every young man into a male model, detracts from what they may want to say about what they do, and creates fantasies.

Many of the magazines have pages of stars caught in embarrassing situations, or have added speech bubbles and captions to celebrity photos. While there is an argument for anyone in the public eye to be 'fair game', some of these are crude, others are nasty and spiteful. There is a streak of cruelty to these pages that demeans others and makes cheap cracks at the expense of those being ridiculed.

 **Action point**

Try to find special interest magazines, Bible notes and books that are attractive and contain fewer worrying elements than general magazines.

Most music and girl magazines have the infamous and popular problem pages, and articles on real-life issues that children and teenagers face. For many readers I am convinced that they provide a forum for them to get advice on many issues that they are afraid to ask about at home, or have no one they can really talk to. Some common themes surface time and time again. The magazines cover bullying, friendships, death, suicide, money problems, issues about school, and a whole range of other topics important to the age group. They also cover relationships, gay issues, sex and contraception advice. Health issues and problems with adolescence and puberty are dealt with sensitively and with facts as well as good advice. The advice given is usually within the law but not within a Christian moral framework. It is often based on a 'feel good' morality – if something feels good or feels right then go ahead and do it. This approach is not supported by a moral framework from Christianity or any other major religion. We looked earlier at the problem of under-age sexual activity, and it is hard not to connect the obsession of these magazines with the fact that many children and young people are sexually active at an increasingly early age.

Action point

Could you provide a question box for the children in your church to use? They could be encouraged to write down any question that they have, place it in the box anonymously, and at an appropriate point leaders and other adults that children trust and respect should answer the questions.

Horoscopes are another feature commonly found in magazines. They follow a fairly formulaic format similar to those in daily or weekly papers, but again the emphasis is on relationships, love and sex.

> The stars tell me what sort of day I will have.

Whether young people take them seriously or not, we should be concerned at the popularity of checking the horoscope as part of everyday life for many children. This flies against God's will and direction for our lives, and many would say is a gateway into a fascination with the occult. But perhaps worse than that, horoscope columns sell dreams to young people who do not have the maturity to cope with the reality that the dream may not come true.

Advertisers use these magazines to sell anything to children. There are the usual items, such as membership of a fan club and make-up kits, to adverts for clothes, banks, mobile phones and videos. The advertisements are often very similar in design to the other pages, and occasionally hidden within an 'advertising feature'.

Books

Despite the growth in the use of the Internet, and against the dire warnings of the pundits, books continue to be a popular form of communication. Books are used at school to help children get into reading and to assist in teaching and research. Christians want children to get excited about the Bible, the only really helpful book for life. Reading is something which many children still enjoy.

The content of books is always a concern for parents and teachers. Theory and text books can generally be relied upon for factual information, albeit from a secular point of view. But fiction books are a different matter. As a child I really enjoyed reading a number of books which were very much in vogue at the time. One particular Alan Garner book, *Elidor*, still sticks in my mind. No other book then or since has grabbed my imagination and made me tingle with anticipation quite like that book did. Now, as I read it from an adult perspective, I am chilled by the depth of evil themes and strange happenings which fill the plot. As a child it was pure fantasy as far as I knew, but now I see it in a different light.

 **Action point**

Find out what children's fiction is available from Christian publishers. Scripture Union has published a book called *Daniel and the Dark Arts* aimed at bringing a wholesome, biblical angle to the Harry Potter phenomenon.

There has been a great debate rumbling on for a few years about the Harry Potter books and subsequent films, and many Christians are concerned that they too are an access point into an unhealthy interest with the world of magic, spells and evil. There has been much written on the subject, and no doubt there will be much more yet. Many of these books and films help and inspire children's imagination in much the same way as pantomime stories about giants, fairies and wicked witches do. C.S. Lewis wrote allegories that were full of such fantasy, which have been made into books and films.

There is no doubt that these books do feature spells, ghosts, evil powers and weird happenings. Whether they are innocent books that help get boys, in particular, reading as many teachers will tell you with glee, or whether they are an evil opening to a satanic world is a question which I am not sure can be answered for everyone. What is evident is that the shelves of any bookshop are now filled with Harry Potter copies and clones, and these may be both not as well written and darker than the originals. Other writers, such as the award-winning Philip Pullman, also cover similar issues but from a much darker standpoint. Pullman has openly stated his opposition to the church and Christianity. His books have an edge of darkness that some children may find disturbing.

Each of us as adults must decide for ourselves where we draw the line, and how we help children who are easily led into unhealthy obsessions and evil fantasies. If in doubt, read the books for yourself and then make a decision.

Investigate the arguments for and against Harry Potter and other similar fantasy themes. The following books may help:

John Houghton, *A Closer Look at Harry Potter* (Kingsway)

Philip Plyming, *Harry Potter and the Meaning of Life* (Grove Books)

Francis Bridger, *A Charmed Life: The Spirituality of Potterworld* (Image)

Connect Bible Study: *Harry Potter* (Scripture Union)

Some books aimed at teenagers and read by children start to unpack themes relating to issues which children face. In this way, they share the territory of magazines. There are great, informative novels about loneliness, peer pressure, marriage breakdown and illness. There are also heaps of books about boyfriends and relationships, again peppered with descriptions of the 'beautiful people' who exist only in books, films and dreams. They can give a message of perfection which can never be attained.

Compile a top ten of books that the children you work with know or read. Ask them about the books, and why they are popular. Try to borrow some of the books to familiarise yourself with what children are now reading.

Computer games

Computer games are popular with many children. They enjoy playing games which have a challenge, and gain a great deal from managing to beat the program or the character they are chasing. Many children now spend as much time playing on computers as they do watching TV. Computer games can be educational in that they aid physical responses and cognitive development. They also serve in many households to keep children quiet for a while. From the earliest age there are programmes available for children, some based on TV programmes, and others with a clear educational aim. Reality is that most children are better at using a keyboard and finding their way around a computer than most adults. Speaking personally, I am useless when attempting to play with my son's Gameboy!

There is an enormous range of games on the market, and what children were playing last year or even last month is likely to have been superseded by a more up-to-date version or a better game. Playstation and Gameboy have another range of games which, as well as being aimed at children, are expensive. Those mentioned by the children surveyed included car racing games, golf, wrestling, and adventure games. Specific titles which featured include *Hogs of War*, *Tomb Raider*, *Heart of Darkness* and *Mission: Impossible*. There were other titles with TV and film tie-ins such as *Pokemon*, *The Simpsons*, and 007. A few children reported not playing any computer games, and others mentioned more basic educational programmes such as *Word and Draw*.

What the children say

There is concern that children who spend a great deal of time playing computer games will suffer in a number of ways. When playing a game they are usually on their own, and therefore they are isolated from family, friends, and society as a whole. There are worries that playing the game to win can become an obsession, and will eat up more and more of the time and energies of the child. This will have an effect on the child's physical health, as they are sitting in front of a computer for much of the time, and will also have a bearing on their ability to form and sustain friendships and relationships with others. There are those who fear that some of the vicious, violent and cruel games have an effect both on the child's understanding of the world around them, and on their grasp of reality. There is an element of cruelty and the macabre in many children, and horror or violent games are popular with children as they work through for themselves what is real and what is not. Over-exposure distorts that balance.

Action point

Challenge the parents in your church to make sure that their Internet settings limit the access children have to 'adult' sites, games and chat rooms.

Some years ago there was concern about the game *Dungeons and Dragons*, which not only seemed to glorify violence, but some asserted could lead children into a sinister world with occult links. The game continues to be played, and there are still fantasy games available which have very dark and sinister themes and content. Again, these are seen as a gateway into a fascination with things of evil.

❝ I spend evenings playing games on the Internet. ❞

A more recent danger of some of these games is that they can lead to contact with other players through the Internet. There are many games sites on the net, and these can easily be used by people with motives against children. Most Internet Service Providers have mechanisms to limit the access children have when browsing, and it is possible to block access to specific sites. But it is not always possible for an adult to be watching everything a child does when playing on a computer or browsing the Internet.

According to the Office of National Statistics, in 2000-01 80% of school children had access to a computer at home, and over 50% also had Internet access. Nearly half of all boys aged 8–15 used a home computer every day, with only 20% of girls doing so. These figures are likely to increase year on year as Internet access becomes commonplace in most homes.

Consider the following questions:

- Should the church be trying to compete with glossy magazines and TV shows?

- If your answer is 'yes', how can you do it, and how much money will it cost?

- If your answer is 'no', what else are you going to offer that will attract children?

Conclusion

Many children enjoy watching programmes with friends and family, and are not obsessed by TV or brought to moral bankruptcy by what they see. Many also enjoy reading books and magazines, may learn a lot of good stuff, and take in what is relevant to them at the time. The increase in computer and Internet use has proved to be a great source of information and has aided the education of many children. But most children are influenced in some way by some of the features of TV, film, magazines, books, websites, and other media. There is much good here, but there is also a little bad too.

The Real World of Image

We all care to some extent about the image we portray to other people. We think about what to wear when meeting special people and hope that people don't notice the dirty old car we go to work in! Image matters in our world, however much we would like to think that it does not matter to us.

I have three styles of clothes depending on what I am doing. If I am attending court in my role as a magistrate, I will wear a formal outfit with jacket and tie. If I am inspecting a school, I will have a slightly more relaxed set of clothes, including a waistcoat and less traditional shoes. If I am in the office or doing an event with children I will wear bright, clashing trousers! There would be nothing worse than misjudging the situation and presenting the wrong image by choosing the wrong set of clothes!

I guess you have heard someone say, when looking at a young couple setting up home together, 'They've got it easy these days. When I was that age we had to make do with what we could get and save up for the rest. Now these young people want everything instantly.' Culture has changed, and it has something to do with image. Image is all about how we look and what we have. In an instant world with a constantly changing set of rules we all want everything instantly. We may be concerned about how our house appears to passers-by or think about getting a new car because it is the oldest on the street.

Children come under the influence of image just as much as adults do. They are under pressure from their peers to behave in a certain way or wear certain clothes. They may be under pressure to get into things which they know they should not do. They are under pressure to spend money, have the latest mobile phone, and look perfect. Danger areas, such as petty crime, smoking, drinking and solvent abuse all rest on image, peer pressure and the fear of being seen as being scared or different.

Action point

Think of the children in your church. What image do you want to portray to them about God, the church, and your faith?

Activities

Image is something that can affect parents. Some parents may try to live their lives again through their children, and thereby put their children under a great deal of pressure. There are so many things that children could be involved in, and sadly some children get drawn into activities not out of choice but because it is what their parents want them to do.

> **❝** I go to clubs every night and at weekends too. I'm never at home! **❞**

Some children live appallingly busy lives. There are vast choices of activities and clubs that children can be involved with after school, in the evenings, at weekends, and during holidays. Many parents find themselves acting as taxi drivers, constantly running their children from one activity to another. Many children find themselves very tired and over-burdened with the pressure of being constantly on the go. But for some they are driven by the need to be seen doing these things, image being the greatest motivator of all.

FACT stop

Make a list of all of the activities available to children in your community, and ask those children you know what activities they are involved in outside school.

In the materialistic culture of our world, children are getting the clear message that it is possible to succeed, and aspirations have been heightened. Children of the current generation are in general much more affluent and confident than those of the past, and see success as being both attainable and measurable in terms of homes, cars and money. This results in children believing not only that the impossible is possible, but also that your worth is measured in terms of what you have, not who you are or what you do.

In research undertaken for the Salvation Army it was found that children are not only under a great deal more pressure to succeed at school and in the job market, but they also have higher expectations of what they will be able to achieve. The prominence of a tiny minority of celebrities who succeed in sport or pop music at a young age suggests to young people that fame and fortune are attainable.

Body Image

Celebrity culture and the obsession with the appearance and dress of those who are famous are sparking a fascination with clothes, fashion and figure. Personal body image is very important in our modern world. Many adults as well as children are concerned about how they look, and the recent rise in the number of gyms and fitness clubs shows no sign of slowing down. There is, of course, nothing wrong with looking after our bodies and working to increase fitness, as long as that is all it is about. I have said much about the beautiful people to be found in magazines and on TV because they project an image of perfection that is not attainable for the majority of us, and for a very few they become an obsession.

❝ I'm really happy when someone makes a good comment about how I look. ❞

Girls have always been keen on make-up and fashion accessories. Now there seems to be a move for children to look glamorous at a very early age. Many people are concerned that the disturbing rise in girls as young as 4 or 5 taking part in beauty contests in the USA will be mirrored in the UK. Primary school discos are fun events, with boys trying to be men and girls trying to be very pretty women. But some of these young girls are allowed to take the challenge too far, and are made up and dressed up to look way beyond their age.

In this image-conscious culture it is an interesting contrast to find that the UK is following in the footsteps of the USA with an increase in the number of children who are overweight and obese. This is considered by many to be the result of a more static lifestyle with less physical activity at school and out of the home. Frequent use of computers, video and TV also contribute to it, along with easy access to fatty convenience foods and fast food from popular outlets. One major chain is now considering publishing the fat content of each meal on the packaging in order to, in their view, 'put the record straight'.

Obesity is considered to be a growing problem in England and Wales. In 1996 13% of children were clinically obese. There is concern that many of these obese children will develop diabetes as a result of their weight. (Office of National Statistics / *Daily Mail*, 27 February 2002)

In Autumn 2002, a number of British newspapers reported that a Californian boy of 10 who has been working out and developing muscle since the age of 2, now has a fully muscular and toned body. His parents are so proud of him that they take him to body-building competitions, and are now teaching his 2-year-old little sister to do stomach-strengthening exercises. The boy spends between two and three hours each day doing exercises and does not attend school.

A few girls, and a tiny but growing proportion of boys, suffer from eating disorders. It is still unclear what all of the causes are, but it is clear that the young people who suffer with such disorders have concerns about their self-esteem and self-image. It would be over-simplistic to say that because they see unattainable images of others that they can never match they try to starve themselves. It would however be reasonable to point out that if these images were a little more realistic and were not selling a visual dream then more young people would be able to relate to them.

Some research from Canada, reported in *The Independent* newspaper, has found that as many as one in four teenage girls suffer from some form of eating disorder. Out of nearly 2000 girls surveyed, 27% had symptoms of binge eating, purging or excessive dieting. Many of the 12–18-year-old girls interviewed had settled into a pattern of disorders by the age of 14.

There is concern that the number of children and teenagers in the UK with eating disorders is growing as a result of the celebrity culture. In a world that studies the shape, size and weight of celebrities there is a pressure to be like them, and a pressure therefore to be slim. There are occasional cases of children and teenagers who have found the pressure too much and have either died from suicide or gradual self-imposed starvation.

Read Psalm 139. How could you use this psalm to communicate to children that image is not important to the God who made us?

In some research by the British Youth Council in 2000 it was found that 57.7% of all girls aged 8–15 said that their appearance was the biggest concern of their lives.

Peer pressure

When I was a child a new board game called *Haunted House* came out. Gradually more and more of my friends got it, until it seemed like I was the only person in the class who didn't. I nagged my parents so much that they gave in and bought it for me on my birthday. I played with it twice and then never touched it again.

Peer pressure exists at all levels of society, from babyhood to old age. Parents of babies are constantly told that this pushchair is best and they are not good parents unless they use that brand of nappies. Children in the world of school, home and community are open to the pressure to conform at an early age.

66 I always do what my friends want me to. 99

Peer pressure can be a good thing. Many schools and classes encourage children to formulate their own school rules and accept ownership. Others have mentoring schemes where younger children are expected to look to older ones for a positive example and role model. This can result in positive pressure from other pupils to follow the rules, with schemes such as 'Playground peacemakers' encouraging peer mediation. A class full of willing children who are listening carefully can be a strong deterrent to the one child who thinks it is funny to disturb their peace with 'rude' noises. Peer pressure operates in a similar way in church groups, Scouts and Guides, and so on.

Negative peer pressure is also a reality for many children. It can range from excluding children from gangs and groups if they don't do certain things, to insisting that friendships are based on the designer label that the child wears on their clothes, more of which later. It is very hard for children to stand out and be different, however wrong they know the actions of others may be.

Action point

Consider the positive peer pressure that the first apostles had on others. To help you, read Acts 2:43-47.

'Everyone was amazed by the many miracles and wonders that the apostles performed. All the Lord's followers often met together and they shared everything they had. They would sell their property and possessions and give the money to whoever needed it. Day after day they met together in the temple. They broke bread together in different homes and shared their food happily and freely, while praising God. Everyone liked them, and each day the Lord added to their group others who were being saved.'

Some churches assume that children find it easy to talk about their church life at school. We may think children will be keen to tell their friends how exciting Sunday School was! We hope that they will invite friends along to church-based events, and won't worry if their friends refuse. The reality is quite different. The majority of children have never set foot inside a church, and can only go on what TV tells them church is like. They get the impression that the church itself is dark and gloomy, with the people inside it being old and miserable. It takes exceptional strength on the part of the child who goes to church to admit to the fact, let alone ask a friend along. And, to be honest, far too many churches *are* dull and boring, and certainly not equipped to cope with children who live in the real world.

 Organise an event at church that is attractive to children, and invest the necessary amount of energy and finance in it. Encourage children to invite their friends, and make sure that it is not an occasion which will embarrass either the church child or their peers.

Peer pressure has an influence over what children wear, what they want to watch on TV and video, what they listen to, what magazines they read, and what they do in their spare time. Peer pressure leads to boys pairing off with girls at a young age, and sexual experimentation for some long before they reach their teens as puberty kicks in earlier. Peer pressure is very powerful.

 Working with a group of children, ask them whether they would throw a stone at a window (a) if they were on their own, or (b) if they were with a group of friends who were 'egging' them on.

Fashion and clothing

My elder son aged 9 has got to the stage where he is beginning to care about what he wears, and there are some items of clothing that no longer see the light of day. The space under his bed seems to have become the clothing graveyard, where items that are not in vogue are left to be forgotten. It is at times like this that I really thank God that he didn't bless me with a girl – I'm not sure I could have coped!

Many of the magazines aimed at the child and teenage market have pages and pages on fashion. There are celebrity photo shoots featuring the latest styles and, more importantly, the right label on the clothes. Children soon get to the stage where what they wear is less important than who made it, and parents can be assured that the labelled goods will be much more expensive than those without labels.

> **❝** I like to wear all the latest clothes. My friends all look the same as me when we dress up to go out. **❞**

This fierce consumer culture is something that has reached the Christian world too. At large Christian events children are targeted as potential consumers of CDs, caps, sweatshirts and other items as used by their favourite worship or celebration leader. It is good for children to take things home with them from such special occasions, but if they are manipulated then the Christian world becomes just as tainted, and just as much a danger to children as the secular one.

When asked what make of clothing and trainers they wear, the answers were fairly predictable. All of the most popular labels and brands were mentioned, including Adidas, Intersport, Quicksilver, Reebok and Nike. Stores mentioned included Tammy Girl, Next and Gap. I was encouraged to find that around 20% of the children, both boys and girls, gave answers such as 'No particular brand' and 'Anything I want to'. Boys were particularly keen to wear sports clothes as much as possible, while girls were keen on sparkly clothes, pinks and purples, and flared jeans.

What the children say

Children have been bullied for not wearing the correct brand of trainers or the right label on their clothes, and this adds to the burden of disadvantage that those from poorer families already have to face. Again, the market experts are relying on the children to do the advertising for them, pestering and nagging hard-pressed parents and carers to purchase the items so that the child can appear right and therefore feel good about him or herself.

The 'youth' economy, based on the spending of children and young teens aged 7–14, is now worth £3 billion per year in Britain. This makes children and young people a major area of purchasing power.

Mobile phones

While thinking about image it would be remiss of me not to mention the mobile. I have a great little blue mobile, and I'm told by some children I know that it is fashionable. It may be so, but for me the buttons are too small and I have to squint to read the text!

> I got a new mobile for my birthday, but I lost it.

In just a few years mobile phones have moved on from being a useful tool for businessmen to being an appendage that many children as well as teenagers and adults must have. There are many different designs, new facilities and abilities including WAP Internet features and texting. Phones can play an array of modern, catchy tunes as ringing tones, and users can send pictures to each other. There are numerous tariffs including paying before use, tokens, top-up cards, and contracts. Children are increasingly using mobiles despite the possible health risks that they may pose.

In England, Wales and Northern Ireland in 2000, 20% of children under 11 owned a mobile phone, compared to 60% of those aged 11 or above. These figures are likely to have increased considerably since then.

There are many good reasons why children should have mobile phones. They are means of communication and can therefore be used to ensure the safety of the user. For example, a carer can get in touch with the child and find out where they are, or the child can call for a lift home or to say that they will be late. But mobile phones also carry risks. There has been an increase in street crime, assault and theft connected with mobile phones in recent years, although most mobile manufacturers and providers have joined together to make it harder for a stolen mobile to be re-programmed and used again. Mobile phone companies, the police and the government are all concerned about how desirable phones are and therefore how popular they are with thieves. There is an obvious danger here for people using or owning such phones, and in particular children who are less able to defend themselves.

" I spend all my money on mobile phone tokens. "

There is also a concern that the radiation given off by mobile phones can affect users. Researchers are not clear about how much damage radiation can cause to the brain, but some are convinced that the frequent use of mobile phones by children, whose brains are still in the development stage, could prove to be very harmful. There are now many promotions and advertisement campaigns aimed at getting young children and teenagers to own and use mobile phones, a method that could be considered irresponsible bearing in mind the dangers.

Texting from mobile to mobile is very popular with children and young people. There is anecdotal evidence that vandalism on school buses has reduced since most children had mobiles, for instead of smashing up the school bus they travel on many children sit on the bus busily texting their friend on the seat behind. Texting helps co-ordination, and we now have a generation of children with the strongest thumb muscles ever. But texting is also antisocial. If a child prefers to send a text than to engage in a conversation they are less likely to develop their social skills.

The Daily Mail reported in October 2001 that the average weekly income for children aged 7–8 was £3.95. In addition, children were increasing their income by doing jobs at home and getting financial gifts at birthdays and Christmas.

Reality

Children are growing up in a world that makes clear to them that everything is possible, and all can attain what they want. It would be a very unwise person who criticised this general aspirational advice, but we all know that it is not as easy as all that. We may have dreams and goals, and some of us may achieve some of them, but for the most part we will have pitched our hopes too high or aimed in the wrong direction. For the majority of us, it takes a very long time to attain our hopes and dreams. This goes against the grain of the instant world in which we live, where everything is expected to happen as quickly as it does in a soap – we become impatient if we have to wait for anything.

Children are open to the suggestion that we should do whatever makes us feel good. TV personalities are seen having a good time and enjoying themselves, and so it is assumed that it is right and good to do the same and have the same attitude. But the feel-good culture leads to self-absorption and inevitable disappointment.

> " I'm going to be rich like (David) Beckham. "

Reality TV and the rise of 'celebrity' have given children, many of them very young, the impression that we can all become very popular, very famous, and very rich very quickly. The interminable TV series to find performers, pop stars and pop groups make it seem as if anyone can do it, and indeed in some cases some very unlikely people have found their few minutes of fame through them. I was watching one such programme recently, where a 16-year-old girl was sent home from the studio after being voted out of the group by her peers. The poor girl and her peers were all devastated by the experience. The girl had to learn rejection, and had to know that she was not considered good enough to continue. But to go through all that on TV in front of an audience of millions strikes me as being at best distasteful, and at worst emotional abuse.

Action point

Use biblical themes and teaching to help children understand the nature of reality. Remind them that out of many thousands of Israelites who left Egypt we only know a few by name, and out of the thousands who followed Jesus only the 12 disciples were mentioned. It is possible that someone in your church will become a superstar, but it is not likely!

What the children say

I recently conducted a session with sixty 10-year-old children on their aspirations. The first question I asked was, 'If you could do any job when you grow up what would it be?' Twenty-seven out of thirty-one boys wanted to be footballers, and nineteen out of twenty-nine girls wanted to be pop stars. I then asked, 'Bearing in mind that it is very unlikely that you will become a footballer or a pop star, what do you think you will do?' This time twenty-four boys were still convinced they would become footballers, with fifteen of the girls still determined to become pop stars. I talked with them after the questions, and in all cases their argument was that it is easy, and they named young people who had succeeded. They were on the whole not willing to accept that, although images of these celebrities were everywhere, there were thousands who had tried and not succeeded. They were yearning after the fame and the money, but not at all convinced about the work that has to go into it.

Reality is, for many children, what they see on the TV. Most homes featured on TV programmes are large, spacious and expensive. So that becomes reality. Those beautiful people are everywhere, on all programmes be they for children, families or adults. So physical attractiveness becomes reality. Most characters on TV programmes, with the exception of some of the more depressing soaps, never worry about money. So free access to cash becomes a reality. The reality that many children live in is far removed from such ideas. Reality culture affects all our children, however hard we try to shield them from it.

Have an intercessory time praying for all the children and young people you know and work with. Ask God to guide them and help them in their hopes, plans and aspirations.

Money

As we have seen, children are a key target area for advertisers not only because of the money they have, but because of the money they can access. Effectively this means all the money that their parents and carers have. The youngest of children are shown images of dolls that cry, dressing-up sets, and action figures, all of which are expensive. As children get older not only do they want the latest games and toys, but they also want to be dressed in the right clothes and trainers, bearing the correct logo and in the latest fashion colour, which for girls is currently purple at the time of writing, but will have changed by the time you read this. The image of reality which children see includes an expensive lifestyle, and children are under pressure from the world and from their peers to have plenty of money and to be able to spend plenty too.

> I want to make lots of money and spend it on things I like.

The money that children spend is often spent on transient things. You would not expect food, drink or magazines to last a long time, but you could be more hopeful about clothes, footwear or cosmetics. However, as fashions change so children feel the pressure to change with them. Music, videos, computer games and the like are all prone to the pressures of fashion, new technologies, special editions and upgrades, all of which cost more money. Even if children have money, they are not likely to have enough to keep up with the rapid changes in the market. But they will want to try.

Consider the teaching your church gives on the reason for and nature of giving. Is it appropriate to encourage children to get into a habit of giving to God? Will teaching on giving help them understand the generosity of a gracious God?

The answers to the question, 'What do you spend your money on?' were no great surprise. The most popular replies were sweets, clothes and accessories, make-up, mobile phone cards and accessories, magazines, CDs and videos. Some children were keen to report that they save all or some of their income, while others mentioned specialist items for air guns, wrestling, horses and Playstation. A few girls generalised by answering with 'girly things', while a few mentioned their boyfriend or girlfriend as the cause of their spending.

What the children say

FACT stop

In 2000-01 children aged 7-15 spent on average £12.30 per week. Girls spent more than boys, and used their money to buy clothing and footwear, and personal goods such as toiletries and cosmetics. Boys spent on average £11.20, using their money on food, soft drinks, and leisure goods such as computer games, CDs and videos.

Action point

Find out more about organisations and agencies that work with and for children and families in poverty.

Visit: Child Poverty Action Group at www.cpag.org.uk

Church Action on Poverty at www.church-poverty.org.uk

The Children's Society at www.the-childrens-society.org.uk

NCH at www.nch.org.uk

The expectation to spend money is all well and good if you have plenty of money to spend! Unfortunately, there are children who fall behind in the image race instantly because they come from families that do not have plenty of money to spend on them. These children stand out in the school playground when there is a non-uniform day or in a school that has no school dress or uniform code. They stand out at the local park or in the street. They are the children who are more likely to be noticed and picked upon for what they wear, what they don't have, and the address at which they live.

In 1998–99 the Office for National Statistics reported that 25% of the UK population was living in poverty. Of these, 35% were children aged under 16. 62% of lone parents are living in poverty.

As a church consider these questions:

Do we as adult members and leaders of the church give a positive example of money management and non-materialistic lifestyles to children?

How do we help our church children stand against the materialistic culture, which is motivated by money?

What can we do to help the families and children in our community who live in poverty?

Conclusion

There is a lot of good in our world. There are positive role models for children to aspire to, and vast opportunities that have not been available to previous generations. There are also traps and temptations which give children the idea that they have to have this or look like that in order to be of value. As ever, there is plenty of good and a little bad too.

The Real World of Church

I was one of those children who attended church from birth onwards, who had good, caring people to lead Sunday School, and who was rooted and grounded in the Bible at an early age. But there were also times at church as a child when I felt excluded and left out. There were moments when everything seemed to be designed for the comfort and happiness of the adults.

There were no specific questions asked about church, and it did not feature at all in the questionnaire responses even when it could have. There was no evidence that, to this cross-section of one thousand children, church had any part to play in their lives, or that church was important. No one reported going to church as a good, enjoyable or fun thing to do. One child wrote about having been in the past but finding it boring.

What the children say

For the sake of this section of the book we will think principally about the children who are in our churches, be they fully involved or hanging around the edges of church life. If we are realistic about the pressures they face and the contradictions they see, we may be able to better address the fact that most children do not see church as having any relevance in their lives.

FACT stop

In a survey conducted amongst five hundred children on one day in March 2000, 93% said that they could not remember ever going into a church apart from with a school group for an educational visit.

Church should be a place, in some cases the one place, where children can feel valued, safe, and loved. Church should demonstrate positive, caring, true family, and real fellowship. Church should not be a place where anyone feels excluded by what is taking place around them.

What children feel about church

As a child I remember leaving Sunday School, which had finished early, and going back into church by accident during the 'Communion'. As it was the custom at the time not to allow children in church for this special part of the service I was mortified, especially when I heard frequent mention of body and blood. I didn't know what was going on, I didn't understand, and I felt frightened and excluded.

Children of today who visit church are less likely to feel fear, but they may well still feel confused and excluded by much that goes on. They will see and hear things which are alien to their experience, and see people doing things which seem amusing or even laughable. Most children don't go to church at all, and have other things to do during the main time that churches meet and provide for them – Sunday mornings.

There have been a number of reports about children and churches. It is notoriously difficult to get up to date and reliable figures on children's Sunday attendance. The Church of England reports that in 2000 there were 180,000 children (under 16) attending a Church of England church on Sunday, with a total of 243,000 children attending church weekly. It is unclear what the non-Sunday attendance was, but it may include parent and toddler groups, midweek children's groups, 'pram' services, and so on (C of E Church Statistics).

The church building

Most church buildings have some history attached to them, be it that they were a factory and have only just opened as a place for a church to meet, or that they have hundreds of years of history. Some children find the whole concept of entering a church building a difficult one. On one occasion I was welcoming a school party to a cathedral when one boy of around 8 burst into tears and refused to enter. It took an experienced teacher four hours to persuade the boy to come in. Talking to him afterwards he said that he was scared of churches because he'd seen funerals and other scary things on TV, and he thought he would die there. Many churches do look gloomy, unwelcoming, dark and frightening. This has always been the case, but as the current generation of children visit them less, they are more likely to retain fears and concerns about the building.

The way some adults treat the church building and expect others to treat it can cause a sense of alienation amongst children. We are good at teaching that God is all around us, yet we also talk of the church as being the 'house of God' and we encourage people to speak in hushed tones when inside. This is a clear contradiction not lost on some children. Perhaps it is right for us to have respect for the building, and perhaps it is appropriate to be quiet in a church, but giving mixed messages about what the building is does not help children. A church building should never become just another building. On the other hand, we are attempting to teach children that God is with us and should be worshipped everywhere, not just in a special, hushed museum.

 **Action point**

Go into your church and look at everything from the level of a child. What can they see, what are they most aware of, and what is outside their vision or understanding? Try walking around on your knees!

The standard of the church building compared to where the children meet and are taught is rarely equal. Some churches are taking their responsibilities to children more seriously, aware that children do not deserve the worst of everything, and that they won't come if they feel they are not getting anything worthwhile. Other churches have some way to go. I have seen children's groups meeting in church towers, kitchens, toilets and broom cupboards. Many groups meet in church halls which range from needing a lick of paint to being damp, dark and rather dingy. I remember getting splinters from the wood-tiled floor of the church hall where I received my Sunday teaching! Meanwhile the main church or worship area is often much smarter, with a great deal of money invested in heating systems, amplification, and sometimes even comfortable seating. There is good lighting, attractive furniture and decoration, and a sense that the space is valued and so are the users of that space. I would not want to suggest that the 'wear and tear' of a space used by children will be the same as one used principally by adults. But that should not be seen as an excuse to do as little as possible to make the area where children meet of a high standard. The message we give children when we send them away to a part of the building that looks unloved and unvalued is that they are unloved and unvalued too.

66 I went to church when I was younger, but I got bored. **99**

Action point

Examine the physical environment in which the children in your church spend their time. Are there any obvious dangers evident, and is the room or area checked by people aware of health and safety guidelines?

Many churches are working hard to make sure that when people do come to church they are welcomed. If we look at the church attendance figures this move is not before time! How children are received as they enter the church, if they are spoken to or not, if they are made to feel welcome, if they are given any of the books and papers, and if there is anything visual that attracts them and draws them in are all factors churches need to think about. The content of the services and what happens after the child is inside the building is the next step, getting them in and making them feel wanted comes first.

Action point

Look at the church diary and list the things that happen during a week or two. Then tick the things you think are accessible to children, and put a cross next to those activities which exclude them. Then ask yourself the question, 'In my church are children really equal partners?'

Church worship

All churches that work with children have different attitudes as to how worship should be conducted when the children are present. Some like to involve children as fully as possible to the extent that the service becomes a children's service and adults feel left out. Other churches barely acknowledge the presence of children at all, or grudgingly throw in a song that they think will keep the children happy. Much has been written about children and worship, including my book *Children CAN Worship*! (Kevin Mayhew), and churches are moving slowly in the right direction. But we still give very mixed messages to the children we try to serve.

There is a language we use in worship that is not accessible to the average adult 'off the street', let alone a child. There are many words, phrases and responses which need a deeper examination before beginning to make sense. Liturgy used in services where children are present needs to be carefully selected and explained to children, not just said because it is always said. For many children and adults who see reading as a difficult or frightening activity, being faced with pages of words is an alienating experience in itself.

The habits and rituals of churches take some learning. For many years I have had the privilege of visiting many churches and a range of denominations, and I am frequently taken by surprise by the way churches do things, and often upset the 'regulars' by getting it wrong, or at least wrong as they see it. Questions I ask range from 'Do you have a procession?' and 'When do you take up the offering?' to 'Do you sing or say the Lord's Prayer?' and 'How do the children leave?' During a church service we stand and sit, speak and listen, move and stay still, turn this way or look there, sing and pray. We do all these things almost automatically because we have learned the system. For many children, coming as they do from a relatively informal school system and not coming across such formality elsewhere, this is mind-blowing stuff. And before we think that this applies to any particular denomination, it doesn't. I remember talking with one of my children after we visited a friend's 'house church'. He asked me, 'Why did they stand still for so long, and do they have to sing those songs so many times?' We all have our rituals, be they ancient or modern!

Action point

Conduct a survey for one month, looking at everything that happens, all the words used, and all the songs chosen for worship while children are present. Mark every element of the service on a scale of one to five, one being unsuitable for children, and five being totally suitable for children. Discuss this with the worship leaders of your church.

When do the children you know sing? The culture of church again seems rather odd to the children of today. Children sing at school, although their willingness often reduces as they get older, and few schools have many children aged 10 or 11 who are keen singers. Children sing along and dance to pop songs and the latest boy band hits, rarely bearing much relation to what we expect them to sing in church. There are some very good worship songs suitable for children, but the assumption that children can only sing action songs, or that 'happy-clappy' lively songs are the only route to take with children in worship, is at best appallingly patronising. Actions can be graceful, moving and relevant, and many slower children's worship songs have BSL sign language actions to them. Children can be quiet, they can sings songs that are reflective and thoughtful, and they can also enjoy jumping around and clapping. Children should be included in worship, and balance is the aim. We should not expect anyone to sing songs which are set to trite tunes, and include classic lines such as 'Ineffably sublime' and 'the trump of the Lord…'. Getting real with children and making worship anything like relevant to them is going to be a long, hard task.

Action point

Conduct a survey amongst the children and families in church for an all-age service. Find out what they enjoy, what they dislike, and what they think would make the worship better.

The church is becoming good at rhetoric about welcoming everyone and being inclusive. The reality is that there are still some areas and activities that are part of worship but from which children are excluded. The classic example of this is excluding children from receiving Communion. Each church or denomination has their own rules and regulations about those who can and cannot receive Communion, with some welcoming children from birth onwards (as was probably the situation until the twelfth century) and others excluding children until they become confirmed or are baptised as adults. I remember causing quite a fuss as a teenager when I requested adult baptism at the age of 14. This was always tied in with automatic church membership, and the church had never been faced with having such a young church member before. To their credit, but after quite a while of waiting while meetings and discussions took place, I was baptised and welcomed as a full, voting member of the church. How many churches have teenagers playing a valid and valuable part in church life, with an input into the growth and worship of the church? Age limits can confuse, leading to undervalued faith, exclusion and a sense of rejection. All age limits for confirmation, believer's baptism, and other important milestones in the life of an individual Christian must take into account that God works with us individually, and he knows what his Spirit is doing better than we do.

Church attitudes

Churches expect children to behave in a way that is completely alien to their culture. There are few, if any, other places and situations in the life of a child where they are expected to sit still (on a hard wooden seat) and listen quietly to someone rabbitting on! A quick few minutes watching the speed and activity of children's TV or observing children as they learn at twenty-first century schools teaches us that we've got a long way to go, and our expectations need to change. Children are able to concentrate, their attention span is not tiny, and we should not necessarily be trying to copy what goes on in the world. But we also have to think through our tired, outdated and 'traditional' approaches. To say, 'It was fine for me in my day to sit still in church' proves the point – that was then, but this is most certainly now, and a now which is a very long way from then. We should have expectations of the children in church, and they must learn what is appropriate behaviour for worship. This may mean knowing when to be quiet and attentive, when to discuss or speak out loud, and when to be active and lively. But this does not necessarily mean always being quiet, subservient, bored or ignored. To expect children to behave during dull sermons, long Eucharistic prayers, and twelve-verse hymns written in an ancient and unintelligible form of our language is as unrealistic as asking adults never to think about their Sunday lunch during the prayers. It may be possible, but is not likely. If all adults behaved in church and didn't whisper, comment, tut at children, mutter, snore or eat sweets it wouldn't be so hard to get children to behave better!

66 I used to go to church, but it was boring and dull. 99

Follow up on children who no longer attend church or church-based activities. Some will have family reasons for not being able to continue, while others may have valid things to say about what is being provided for them.

Children finding faith

Children's groups should be places that are models of quality work, where children are truly valued, teams of workers are properly trained, and a range of skills is demonstrated. What message do we give to children when the children's work is of a poor quality, and when the church work with children is very low in the church's priorities? Children have all too often been subject to second-rate teaching from people who are under-resourced and under-valued in their ministry to children. The message they so often receive is that they are not really wanted and they just make work for others and cost money. Children would be justified in asking why adults get comfortable chairs, good paperwork and books, OHPs and even PowerPoint visuals, while they get badly photocopied worksheets! In many churches it simply is not good enough, and the culture of church rejects children.

I hope most churches that work with children want those children to find a personal faith for themselves. While we talk about God working in all of our lives in different ways, there are some churches that put a strong pressure on children to 'make a decision'. While it is right to encourage young people to have a living faith for themselves, too much emphasis on this can either scare them away or force them into a false declaration of faith for a bit of peace. Other churches tend to shy away from such clarity and assume that all children have started on their journey of faith – they do not have any will to think or talk it through. These churches confuse children by filling them with head-knowledge but giving them no opportunity to turn it into heart-faith.

The best way to help children develop their own spiritual lives must be to allow God, through his Spirit, to move and sow seeds that will grow in God's time rather than plant ideas and feelings that may not be real, genuine or life-changing.

Action point

What does your church think about children and their personal faith development? It is worth looking at books and resources that will help your church and children's work teams think this issue through further.

Ron Buckland, *Children and the Gospel* (Scripture Union)

David Hay and Rebecca Nye, *The Spirit of the Child* (Fount)

Francis Bridger, *Children Finding Faith* (Scripture Union/CPAS)

Churches that talk openly about allowing children and young people to play a full part in church life need to think through how much consultation actually takes place. If children are the church of today they must be able to contribute to the shaping and development of that church. After all, children are part of it now, not growing into it. The church must accept the voice of children and keep it in balance with all the other pressure groups represented in the church family.

Children from church families are very blessed in many ways, but suffer too. If a parent is taking the Sunday School group it is possible that their own child will be treated more harshly than the others, and will get another helping of discipline in the car on the way home. They may also have to face the teasing and bullying of other children who think going to church is wet, and suffer from not being able to do the things their friends are doing on Sundays. If we make the church experience too painful for our children they will choose another way of life, or another culture to follow.

Action point

Write down the minimum or average ages that children have to be for rites of passage, church membership, leading worship, adult confirmation or baptism, preaching, and so on in your church. Are there rules, be they hidden or set down, which need to be challenged in order to make church culture more accessible and attractive to children?

FACT stop

The Christian Research website reports that Sunday church attendance in Great Britain is falling in all age groupings, with a drop from 5,441,000 in 1979 to 3,714,700 in 1998.

Action point

Consider your church's long-term approach to reaching and serving children. Bring in someone to help the church work through the issues, perhaps a diocesan or denominational worker with a specialism in children's work, or a worker from Scripture Union, Children Worldwide or another organisation.

Conclusion

The church, like any other social grouping, has its own ways of doing things that can appear strange, eccentric and confusing. This church culture is principally designed by adults for adults, and therefore ignores a significant sector of the congregation, and a potentially massive growth area. If that's how we want it then let's go ahead. Then when we're on our last legs we can have very quiet services with no disturbances, no noise, and no concessions to other generations. We can be as selfish and mean with our worship and our faith as we like. And as we die out the Christian church will die out with us.

But it doesn't have to be like that! The church of Jesus Christ is supposed to be a dynamic, vibrant witness to the culture around it. We're positively encouraged to be radically counter-cultural, to have fun and to demonstrate life to the full. If we really took that to heart we could be very attractive to children.

Conclusion

Kids' culture is fast-moving, stimulating and exciting. It presents children with unimaginable opportunities to live and learn. The majority of children today will grow up to be better educated, better nourished and better informed than any previous generation.

Kids' culture is also worrying, dangerous and challenging. Everyone who works with children needs to be aware of and take seriously what the world offers to them, and to think creatively, in the wisdom of the Spirit, about how we can protect and equip children to better face the worst excesses of their culture.

Action point

Read and consider Mark 9:42. What does it have to say to those who endanger or seek to manipulate children?

'It will be terrible for people who cause even one of my little followers to sin. Those people would be better off thrown into the sea with a heavy stone tied around their necks.'

An examination of kids' culture leaves us as the church with many challenges. Hopefully, by working through the Action points in this book, you will have discovered some of those that are most relevant to your particular situation. Only our best will do for God and for the children he has placed in our care, whether we are parents, church leaders or simply members of a congregation. How we deal with the children who come into contact with our church is a vital part of our conduct as Christians. Do we give the children in our churches the value they deserve? This may be demonstrated by the place in which our children's groups meet, our careful (or otherwise) choice and vetting of children's group leaders and our child protection policy, or simply by the time that we give to listen to and appreciate the problems and joys that the children face.

In the end we can only do a little, but for individual children in our care or under our influence that little could be everything! This is God's world, and the children are his. They are precious to him, and he loves them with an intensity we cannot come close to understanding. In all the fear and darkness of our world we also see his healing and know that the light of Christ shines, often using the words, actions or smiles of children to do so! We are aware of the dire consequences promised for those of us who damage the developing faith of children, and we know that as the church we have to make a stand and develop an example of counter-culture which children can see is worth following. Just imagine how your community could be changed if all of the children in your church became disciples, apostles, and evangelists! I hope this book has helped you to become more aware of the issues, and given you a renewed vision to make a difference.

All is not lost! The last word in this book should go to the children themselves, who live in their own culture and face all of these pressures. May God bless them, and all who work with them to help them meet God.

When asked 'What would you do to change the world?' nearly all of the children gave answers that revealed an understanding of the good and bad of their world, and a concern for others. Here are some of the main themes:

What the children say

Get rid of bad news, and celebrate good things.

Make sure that everyone has enough to eat and drink.

Change schools and give us long holidays.

Remove all poverty and make sure no children are poor.

I wouldn't allow smoking or alcohol.

I would pay teachers more money.

Stop animal killing and testing things on them.

There would be no litter and no damage to things.

I would destroy all drugs.

Everyone would have to be really kind and helpful.

There should be a ban on racism and homework!

There would be no war or suffering.

All girls should get married aged twelve.

I would get rid of crime and turn bad people into good guys.

The ozone layer would be saved.

Everything!

I would do all I could to make it a better, friendlier place.

We could read up on the culture of children for ever, but now we need to get on and help children cope with it and become part of an effective and attractive counter-culture themselves. Have fun!